Dreams & Dreaming
Understanding your Sleep Messages

Alternatives
Life Options for Today

Dreams & Dreaming
Understanding your Sleep Messages

TONY CRISP

First published in Great Britain in 1999 by
LONDON HOUSE
114 New Cavendish Street
London W1M 7FD

Copyright © 1999 by Tony Crisp
The right of Tony Crisp to be identified as author of
this work has been asserted by him in accordance with the
Copyright, Designs and Patents Act, 1988

This book is sold subject to the condition that it shall not,
by way of trade or otherwise, be lent, resold, hired out
or otherwise circulated without the publisher's prior
written consent in any form of binding or cover other
than that in which it is published and without a
similar condition including this condition being imposed
upon the subsequent purchaser.

A catalogue record for this book is available
from the British Library

ISBN 1 902809 07 6

Edited and designed by DAG Publications Ltd, London.
Printed and bound by Biddles Limited,
Guildford, Surrey.

For Chris

Your life is more than a day. It is more than a year. It includes a thousand hopes, countless pleasures and pains beyond memory. Your life is not even your own, but a vast, wonderful weaving of many others into your being. Even the animals and landscapes, the houses you have loved or feared, are intricately a part of you. Shall a painting capture you, or words, or a photograph tell all that you are? No. Only your dreams can display the mystery of your years, and the many things your life has brought forth.

Contents

Introduction 8
1. Dreams — Doorway to Wonder 9
2. Where Do Dreams Come From? 21
3. Science v. Experience and Religion 37
4. Travels in Virtual Reality 59
5. Dream Meanings 79
6. Destiny and Dreams 97
7. Dreams: The Final Frontier 119
8. Dream Questions Answered 135
Dream Resources 148
Notes 151
Index 157

Introduction

In the pages of this book you will discover:

- How dreams can reveal aspects of your mind, body and spirit.

- How the language of dreams is like any other, and that understanding its structure, idioms and metaphors enables you to be clear about what dreams mean.

- That the findings of science and the personal experience of dreams are not in conflict.

- How you can enter the virtual reality of your dreams while awake, and communicate with dream characters and creatures to unfold the amazing information they hold.

- How to stimulate or 'incubate' a dream to give practical help in solving problems of work, relationship or creativity.

- What lucid dreams are and how to enter their profound new dimension of experience. How to plan and attempt an out-of-body experience.

- Why you have recurring dreams, nightmares or walk in your sleep.

- What really lies behind the terrors of sleep paralysis.

- How to make the dream journey toward discovering your wholeness and part in the scheme of things.

1
Dreams – Doorway to Wonder

The Mystery Of Dreams
You sleep for about a third of your life. Most of that period is spent in one form of dreaming or another[1]. This means that if you sleep for an average of seven hours a day and live seventy-five years, *twenty-two years of your life are spent dreaming!*

Human life is strange and mysterious. Because dreams display the workings of the mind and imagination, they are among the most mysterious and fascinating aspects of your life. Writing about the complexity and scope of the human brain, Tony Buzan, the inventor of 'Mind Maps', says that even comparing it with the vastness and intricacy of a galaxy is a modest analogy. This is because your three-and-a-half pound brain mass contains about ten billion nerve cells.

Each of these can link with any of the others through patterned connections that outnumber in scope the atoms in the universe. As you think, experience and feel responses, as creativity expresses itself, your brain flashes through this unimaginable number of patterned connections thousands

> **WHAT IS A DREAM?**
>
> There are many definitions of dreams. They range from an ancient view of them being messages from the gods through to the idea of dreams as windows to your unconscious feelings and thoughts. A modern stance regards dreams as neurological and chemical events.
>
> However much one tries to fit the enormous range of dream phenomena into any one or several of these definitions, there is never a complete match. Is a dream a piece of drama? Is it a psychological event? Shall we view the dream from a spiritual stand or think of it as chemical reactions?
>
> Because we can see dreams from any of these viewpoints, like any life experience dreams are transcendent. They transcend all attempts to give them a final definition. There is always an element that remains indefinable.

of times each second. This is beyond your normal ability to imagine, despite the fact it is happening to you.

The human mind has immense possibilities. We see this in the extraordinary things people do, either in their everyday lives or in times of crisis. We know from laboratory evidence that individuals can consciously slow their heartbeat, change body temperature, solve mathematical problems as fast as any computer or heal themselves of illness. Dreams involving the unwilled or willed action of the brain during sleep express and often unveil much more of the vastness of these inner resources than are usually accessible while awake.

The Many Facets of Dreaming

There is no final agreement on what dreams are and what is their value. But they can be seen to hold in them something of all the aspects of human life. Just as society has hospitals, churches, schools, libraries and sports facilities to cater for the physical, spiritual,[2] mental and recreational needs of people, so dreams express these various facets of yourself.

● *Body Dreams* — Bernard S. Seigal, MD, Assistant Clinical Professor of Surgery at Yale University School of Medicine, originated the 'Exceptional Cancer Patient' group therapy. By encouraging his patients to tell their dreams and express feelings through paintings, he found that they often dreamt clearly about the condition of their body long before normal diagnostic methods could define the illness or healing. Other physicians, such as Kasatkin in Russia, have also drawn notice to this aspect of dreaming, keeping careful records of patients' dreams.

● *Virtual Reality* — Sigmund Freud recognised that dreams are different in quality to waking fantasies or day-dreams. While dreaming you are usually convinced that your surroundings and what happens are completely real. This sense of total immersion in the dream does not pervade waking fantasies. Although during a nightmare this feeling of reality can cause you to be very frightened, the positive side is that dreams give an experience as full of impact as waking life, and are therefore as educational.

● *Regulating* — In experiments where volunteers were woken each time they began to dream, a breakdown in the efficiency of mind and body soon became apparent. The Swiss psychiatrist Carl Jung described dreams as 'compensatory'. He was particularly referring to the way they help balance your conscious personality. According to this view, any extreme of feeling or attitude is compensated for by an expression of the opposite in dreams. Apart from compensating in this way, dreams also appear to be essential in keeping the personality in balance and for psychological growth in general. Just as there are self-regulating processes in your body helping it to grow or survive, so dreams play a similar part for your personality.

- *Personal Growth* — The growth of the personality from infancy is a very complex interplay between largely unconscious factors in your body, experience of environment and the way you integrate and deal with these different influences. Dreams appear to present clear indications of what you are facing in your present growth. They reveal past experience that through trauma may need to be met in order to live life in a more satisfying or efficient way. This is why dreams are so often used in psychotherapy. Because your mind integrates experience, some investigators believe that during dreaming you 'upgrade' skills such as social interaction, speech and creative action. This also produces personal growth.

There is neurological evidence that brain cells undergo a learning process during dreaming. In the area of personal growth, inquiry into dreams such as recurring nightmares shows them to be an attempt to bring to consciousness and release past traumas, such as abandonment in childhood, involvement in war environments or car accidents. What is most important is that dreams can be a pathway to finding a greater sense of who you are in the world and of discovering your relationship with the world around you. Through dreams, you can gradually be initiated into the experience that your fundamental self is eternal and part of all life.

- *Creativity* — In 1912, Max Wertheimer launched Gestalt psychology in Germany by publishing a paper on a visual illusion called 'Apparent Motion'. Wertheimer noticed that when we view a sequence of still pictures, such as watching a film, we have the illusion of seeing movement. This was different to the perception of its components — the many static images.

This led to the understanding that a high proportion of the perceptions we have of the world around us — and many of the concepts we build — are radically different to the countless pieces of information or experience from which they arise. The sum is therefore different to or greater than the parts. When seen from this point of view, sudden inspirations and creative leaps are usually a new 'whole', formed of many parts that previously had no connection. The symbols and drama of dreams particularly express this creative forming of new skills and realisations — new gestalts — that arise out of the mass of separate pieces of experience or information.

● *Imagination* — This has been listed separately to creativity because they are not necessarily the same. Imagination has been described as the 'ability of the mind to be creative or resourceful'. To be creative or resourceful is considered highly admirable yet being imaginative is frequently regarded as a waste of time. Most of the greatest things in the external world arose out of imagination. Such inventions as vacuum cleaners and pictures that could be sent through the air — TV — seemed outlandish to logical, rational people when they were first mentioned. Dreams are possibly the most powerfully imaginative experiences we can have. Through them we can break free of the restrictions and lack of perception our logical mind may have.

● *Exercise for the Psyche* — Freud believed that dreams express repressed desires, such as sex and anger. Jung said that in dreams we compensate for what is not experienced in our life. Seen in a more positive light, we can each see that our daily life only allows us to live a small range of the events we would like or need to do or feel. The circumstances of our life may lead us to prevent ourselves from expressing openly the intensity of the love, pain, anger and creativity within.

In dreams, such restrictions fall away to some degree. Our mind, emotions and sexuality unfold and we can discover a fuller range of expression and capability. Howard Roffwarg, a psychiatrist at Columbia University in New York, suggested that nervous activity during REM (i.e. rapid eye movement or dreaming) sleep helps to stimulate the developing brain in very young children, thus promoting the growth of neural connections necessary for learning. In adults, according to Roffwarg, REM serves, like physical exercise, to maintain tone in the central nervous system.

● *The Supersenses* — Sensitive instruments tell us that your eyes only see a small range of the colour spectrum, missing infra-red and ultra-violet, for instance. Your ears hear only a portion of the sound scale. But your mind, through your senses and emotions, can extrapolate from the thousands of pieces of information you take in. For example, if you look at a person for a few minutes you might have few thoughts about what type of individual they are. But if questioned carefully, you will realise that you have very definite impressions about them from the way they dress, stand, talk and move. In fact, you 'know' a great deal about him or her. In dreams, you not only browse through and build insight or knowledge from the huge amount of information you have taken in, but sometimes leap right beyond what your senses have enabled you to gather, and arrive at true intuitive perception.[3]

Considering these many aspects of dreaming, what a waste of a wonderful resource, what criminal negligence it is, if you fail to remember dreams and gain enrichment from their fresh and unique perspectives. What a loss if you do not discover their pungent comments on your relationships and their possible outcome, and the opportunities dreams present to explore new approaches to everyday life. What a denial of potential if you do not discover the many-splendoured facets of your mind and consciousness. As Robert van de Castle says: 'You were issued a lifetime pass to free dreams at birth. Why not take advantage of it?'[4]

There is not space to give examples of the ways in which your dreams deal with the many different dimensions of your being. However, below are some explanations and illustrations of just how powerful and varied they can be.

You Dream Virtual Reality

Research carried out by the Department of Philosophy in Turku University, Finland, suggests that both dreams and the everyday phenomenal world may be thought of as constructed virtual realities. Recent neurological findings show how the brain constructs a sense, or view, of reality out of your sense impressions and cultural/personal values. Reality is different to what you see, hear or believe. In your dreams you can create unlimited types of reality. The wonder of this is that you can explore experiences with which you might be too timid to experiment in waking life. Some ideas about how the human mind interacts with reality suggest that you actually create the world around you similarly to the way you do in dreams.[5]

While I was working for Teletext in the UK I received a number of dreams illustrating these ideas. This first one is from Sandra. She was sixteen at the time.

> I enter the pub from *'EastEnders'* and see Sarha Mitchell, a US actor I find attractive. I fancy him, and decide to attract him by adjusting my clothes to reveal plenty of cleavage. I approach him so he can ask me what I would like to drink. He is looking down at my breasts and is suddenly interested in me. We begin to chat and make a date.

Here is another one from Joanne:

> I dreamt I was heavily pregnant and naked, lying on the floor of a dark room with one light directed on me. My former boy friend was next to me, naked, stroking my hair, telling me everything was going to be all right. In the dream I felt physically sick, but inwardly perfectly calm and at peace. But I am confused as I am only fifteen and there is no chance I'm pregnant.

Within the virtual reality of her dream, Sandra is experimenting with her ability to attract a man using physical appeal. Having tried this out in her dream, Sandra may or may not use this in everyday life. The dream Joanne describes is common among young women. It involves either being pregnant or actually giving birth. In both cases, it is a way of gaining confidence and meeting anxieties about the possibility of pregnancy. It allows the dreamer to gain experience in an area that would be difficult, painful or dangerous to experiment with in waking life. In this and many other ways, dreams allow you to explore without the risks you would meet in waking life.

You Dream Problem-Solving

All of us face and solve countless problems each day. They include everything from how to open a cupboard door to wrapping a parcel or finding a telephone number. However, some situations you encounter are not easily resolved. Sometimes these difficult problems are only resolved when you access information or insights that are usually unconscious or not reached by rational thought. Possibly you have apparently forgotten the piece of information that would solve the difficulty. Such necessary information, new views or totally different experience can be reached in the virtual reality of dreams.

Here is an excellent example of this. It appeared in the 27 June, 1964, edition of the *San Francisco Chronicle*.

The golfer Jack Nicklaus had a long period of bad performance. He spent a lot of time trying to analyse what he was doing wrong, but this did not help. He then had a dream in which he was holding his golf clubs differently. This led to his swings feeling perfect. He told a reporter: 'When I came to the course yesterday morning, I tried it the way I did in my dream and it worked . . . I feel kind of foolish admitting it, but it really happened in a dream.' From that time on his performance improved rapidly.

You Dream the Body
In the early nineties a friend, Ken S, came to consult me in my capacity as a dream therapist. He experienced a dream that troubled him and wanted to understand it. In the dream, Ken was walking along the upstairs passageway of a large, old house. He was in his dressing-gown on the way to the bathroom. About halfway along the passage, he felt a fine spray of water on his body. This drew his attention to a small leak in a large water pipe running along the passageway. At that very moment, the pipe burst and a torrent of water poured out. Ken was then rushing around trying to deal with the burst pipe, but fire also started elsewhere in the house.

Ken and I approached the dream using a traditional psychotherapeutic method in which each aspect represents an emotion or psychological state. We did not get any satisfaction with this so ended with the view that we had not discovered the associations and powerful feelings that would uncover the hidden parts of Ken's psyche. Three days later, Ken was rushed into hospital with a burst colon. He was near to death, but with surgical and medical help recovered. When I next saw him, still in hospital, our eyes met and we both said at the same moment, 'The dream!', meaning it had been a warning of the burst colon.

Despite being involved in dreamwork with groups and individuals, and having read about how some dreams express physical conditions, I had never previously been so directly confronted by such a dream. Now I am much more alert to this possibility. Dream dictionaries may have their limitations, but if this dream had been looked at in the basic way such books define, Ken would have sought medical attention sooner.

For instance, *House* can represent yourself or your body. *Water-Pipe* may depict your intestines or arteries while *Fire* means consuming passions, an emergency or illness. Because of the context of the different dream images, Ken's dream points to physical breakdown.

Although Ken's body dream is about illness, such dreams are not limited to showing what is going wrong inside us. They often indicate positive health changes, or may be about which foods best suit us or cause harm.

ARE MY DREAMS DENOTING ILLNESS?

In considering dreams to look for signs of illness, it must be remembered that most people at some time experience awful dreams in which they are stabbed or bitten, or are near to fire or war. Many of us dream of a part of our body being deformed or sick.

In the majority of cases, these refer in some way to your emotions, fears, personal growth or social life. Only when there is a very persistent and pervading quality about such dreams should they be taken to indicate the possibility of illness. At such time, seek medical help to confirm or deny the message of the dreams.

You Dream the Supersenses

The question of whether we have supersenses is disputed in some scientific circles. Joseph Bullman, director of *The Secrets of Sleep*, a recent UK Channel 4 TV series, gives an interesting comment on this. While researching the series, Bullman travelled to America. Searching through books on dreams in the Los Angeles Public Library, he saw an entry called 'Psychic Dreams' that caught his eye. It was in a book titled *The Encyclopaedia of Sleep and Dreaming*. The passage read:

> A woman who described herself as having frequent out-of-body experiences spent several nights being monitored in a sleep laboratory. One night she awakened from sleep and correctly reported a five-digit number that had been placed out of sight on a high shelf above her bed. She reported that she saw it while floating above her body.

Bullman's aim for the series was to report in a popular way what the experts knew and did not know about the subjects of sleep and dreams. In reading about a woman who was observed in laboratory conditions to read a hidden five-digit number while asleep, he wondered why the experiment was not famous. Why was it not seen as an enormous breakthrough, like Crick and Watson's discovery of DNA structure? After all, the implications of what the woman did are astonishing!

It took Bullman six months to discover who did the experiment and track him down. In visiting sleep-lab after sleep-lab nobody had even heard of the experiment. Then one of his researchers found mention of it in an obscure academic journal. The author was Dr Charles T. Tart who wrote the book *Altered States of Consciousness*.[6] Tart wired 'Miss Z' — the subject — to an EEG machine to watch her brain-wave patterns as she slept. He took a random number, wrote it on a piece of paper, sealed it in an envelope, climbed a step-ladder and placed the envelope on a shelf high above Miss Z's head.

On the first three nights Miss Z reported that she had not been able to leave her body to view the envelope. On the fourth night, she said she had managed, and correctly told the number — 25132. Tart also instructed Miss Z to look at the clock on the wall when she experienced leaving her body so he could check this against the EEG reading. He describes the reading as '. . . unlike anything anyone had seen before. The brain-wave recordings on the EEG appeared to show that when she saw the five-digit number, her brain was both awake and asleep at the same time.'[7]

Not only does Tart's experiment with Miss Z show there is a physiological and neurological basis for an out-of-the-body experience — OBE — but also illustrates how, in Bullman's words, '. . . scientists who come up with results that challenge conventional beliefs are ostracised by the academic establishment. This work, I discovered, did indeed have revolutionary implications for mainstream science. And, precisely because of this, it had been all but ignored.'

You Dream Self-Regulation

Anthony's Textbook of Anatomy and Physiology uses the word *homoeostasis* to represent the body's ability to maintain and heal itself. It says:

> The principle of homoeostasis is one of the most fundamental of all physiological principles. It may be stated in this way: the body must maintain relative constancy of its chemicals and processes in order to survive. Or stated even more

briefly: health and survival depend upon the body's maintaining or quickly restoring homoeostasis.

Without this self-regulatory or homoeostatic process in your body, you would be dead within a very short period of time. Perspiration is part of self-regulation; without it you would not lose heat fast enough and some of your tissues would fry. Your heart wouldn't speed up as you moved, while the brain would find itself starved of oxygen, and so on. After working with patients awakening from a coma-like state lasting for years, Dr Oliver Sacks observed this self-regulatory process at work in their efforts to adjust to life once more.[8] He says, 'We have to recognise homoeostatic endeavours at all levels of being, from molecular and cellular to social and cultural, all in infinite relation to each other.'

What Sacks observed — and what some aspects of modern psychology often reject — is the process of self-regulation (SR) working in our mind and psyche as well as in the body. Dreams are one of the main processes in the self-regulation of the psyche. My observation of this process over the past thirty years has led me to define the action of SR as:

● The major and natural process in us dealing with healing of physical and psychological problems.

● Through dreams and fantasy, the self-regulatory process confronts us with experiences and information our waking personality may be avoiding. Emotions, such as resentment or grief, that have been suppressed can cause illness if persistently denied expression. Through psychosomatic processes, and unwilled movements and tensions, SR presents information about our state of body or mind. If we fail to recognise this consciously, our dreams will portray them.

● The main creative process of the unconscious. It can enrich our work and relationships. This is because SR underlies all our processes of growth, physical or psychological. For instance, it was the 'hand at the helm' when we gained weight to the extent of twenty-seven million times as we grew from sperm/ovum to birth. Current psychological theory does not yet accept that such deeply cellular processes can be known consciously. Yet researchers have witnessed people able to slow their heart or change their body condition.

● A way of expressing or exploring all the levels of our being, including everything from physiological processes and physical movement, through non-rational feelings and concepts, to the emotions and rational thought that lead to insight.

● An initiation of our waking consciousness to experiences beyond the limitations of our senses and personality. When we are ready, SR introduces us to a sense of the huge collective and interlinked forces and living being in which we are an integral part.[9]

Dreams in which this process of self-healing or personal growth appear are sometimes similar to problem-solving ones. However, they usually deal more with emotions and attitudes. This following dream is an excellent example. It was told to me during a talk given to The Housewives' Register in Ilfracombe.

My mother-in-law died of cancer. I watched the whole progression of her illness, and was very upset by her death. Shortly after she died, relatives gathered and began to sort through her belongings to share them out. That was the climax of my upset and distress. I did not want any part of this sorting and taking her things.

That night, I dreamt I was in a room with all the relatives. They were sorting her things, and I felt my waking distress. Then my mother-in-law came into the room. She was very real and seemed happy. She said for me not to be upset as she did not at all mind her relatives taking her things. When I woke from the dream all the anxiety and upset had disappeared. They never returned.

Dreams in which the SR process is evident usually attempt a change — or give you experience of the change — as in the quoted dream. Because of this, SR is very much an underlying process in nightmares. Unfortunately, although the fears are met in a nightmare, they are often not fully felt so no satisfying conclusion is reached. In trying to complete unfinished internal business, SR seeks to deal with past traumas and personality traits that stand in the way of growth. The attempt may not always be successful as we might pull back from the disturbing emotions or 'work' involved. If this seems strange, we must remember that as humans we are perverse. The very acts that might be of greatest good, like stopping smoking, may be those we do least. Our habits of pain-avoidance or repression of emotions often stand in the way of SR completing itself. This is why a conscious decision to explore your dreams aids such healing.

These are just a few of the different areas of experience dreams take us to. Your dreams will be even more varied and personally exciting. In the next chapters, we will look at what a dream is, how to enter its world and how to bring back treasures of insight.

2
Where Do Dreams Come From?

Where do dreams come from? Why do we often have the same dream or dream scene over and over? How come dreams are so obscure and difficult to understand? What does it mean when you dream about the sea, an animal or sex? Can dreams predict the future?

To help understand these questions it is worth looking at some very strange dreams, the reason being that they are examples of the most basic processes active in dreams. For instance, why are Janice and Mrs Jones paralysed and terrified in the following dreams? What is happening to them?

> I am lying on my back. I feel completely conscious, but cannot move. I become terrified that I might suffocate under the duvet, and that I would have to lie there until somebody came along to move me. I have had this dream for years. I used to think it was not a dream, and as I slept on my stomach, trained myself only to sleep on my back or side in case I suffocated. Recently, I woke from the experience so realise it is a dream. The fear lasts through the day. I even dread going back to bed.

Mrs Jones, who described this dream, is not alone in her terror of the night and its dreams. What she details is a common experience. Here is another example from Janice P:

> I am lying semi-conscious in bed when this horrible force pulls my body out of bed into mid-air. I can see this happening and try to shout, but no noise can come out. I am watching myself lifting, but I have not moved at all. I see my arm lying on the bed, yet I am lifting it up. I fight the force and manage to win.

In times past, Janice and Mrs Jones might have believed that an evil spirit, an incubus or succubus, had taken control of their body and soul while they slept. Such beliefs were common, being attempts to explain the often inexplicable experiences individuals met in sleep and dreams. Because we all inherit some of the ways people thought about things in the past, this feeling of evil may still persist in our dreams today. Mandy described her dream in these words:

> When upset, I dream I am in a large room or at the top of a long flight of stairs. It is dark. I feel a force pulling me down the stairs or to another room. The force pulls me, although I know there is evil. I say 'No! No!' and fight it. I wake when I am flying fast towards the evil and cannot breathe.

As can be seen from Mandy's dreams, she meets the force that moves her against her will, and feels it is evil. Modern sleep laboratories, with equipment sensitive enough to register brain activity as well as body responses, have begun to give us clear insight into just what is happening to Mandy. They have thrown light into the mysteries of dreams and the strange world of sleep. From this information we can now begin to find answers to age-old questions.

Foundations in Understanding Dreams

To gain personal understanding of what happens when you dream, there are a few basics you need to know. Without this information dreams and sleep experiences, such as those of Janice and Mandy, can appear mysterious, ridiculous or even terrifying. With the information, you not only have clearer insight into your own experiences of sleeping and waking, but feel more confident about who you are. The insights gained are also important in understanding dreams in general. The basic pointers to know are:

● When we sleep, our body and brain are in a *very* different condition than when awake. Judging what happens in sleep from the standpoint of waking is as ridiculous as assessing adult behaviour from a child's emotional maturity. Looking at what happened to Janice from what we know about waking life creates fear.

● The process that causes us to dream creates fantastically realistic hallucinations. In previous pages I used the words 'virtual reality'. But neither 'virtual reality' nor 'hallucinations' properly convey what we meet in dreaming. When she read the five-figure number, Charles Tart's subject, Miss Z, was not seeing a virtual reality. Nor was she hallucinating. She was experiencing reality, but perhaps a different order of reality. It is nevertheless important to realise that *the dreaming process can create what has been called hallucination — the conviction that we are seeing a real person or scene outside ourselves, or experiencing a real event.* Once you appreciate this, seeing ghosts with eyes open, or other strange visual or auditory experiences, also become understandable.

● Dreams employ imagery in the same way our everyday language utilises images to express what we feel and think. Dreams also reflect our thought processes. For instance, how many meanings can you attach to the words 'Blue', 'Dog', 'Bridge' or 'Flying'? As an example, we can put potatoes in a sack, get the sack or sack a city. We can fly in an aeroplane, fly into a rage or see a fly. We also commonly use puns, allusions or associational connections to convey meaning, criticise or make a joke. We have an innate sense of drama and the feeling tone of visual or auditory 'scenes'. This enables us to enjoy watching a film and be emotionally or intellectually moved by a shift in lighting, a subtle alteration in facial expression or costume, or a changed musical background.

Dreams use all these in a quite blatant and incredibly skilful manner, but graphically rather than verbally. If we fail to understand a dream, it may be because we have not observed our own allusions, our own verbal imagery, and our own sense of drama and scene. After all, does a dark raining sky in grey city streets convey the same message as bright sunshine in a colourful beach setting?

● Dreams are in no way any less meaningful, no less an expression of your past, your totality or your human condition, than any other tiny, wonderful part of your life. The more we learn about our body and mind, the more we realise what exquisitely functional and amazing creatures we are. Every tiny cell is meaningful and has a place in the scheme of your body and mind. Each cell, organ or system interacts and interrelates with all the others. Your past, whether genetic, social or personal, directly relates to who you are and what your condition of mind and body is today. You are therefore a part of the scheme of things, directly linked to all that has happened and all that will happen. In fact, your dreams are doorways into the wonder that you are.

Entering the Caverns of Sleep and Dreams

Let us take each of these fundamentals and unfold the information still further.

1. *When we sleep, our body and brain are in a VERY different condition than when awake.*

Basically, when we are asleep we are less active. But there are at least two sorts of sleep. One has been defined as NREM (non-rapid eye movement), and the other as REM (rapid eye movement). The latter is best known because it has been recognised for longer. In 1937, through the use of the electroencephalograph, Loomis and his associates discovered that the forms of brain waves change with the onset of sleep. The next leap forward in understanding came when Eugene Aserinsky found rapid eye movements in 1953. Aserinsky was a University of Chicago graduate student at the time, and was testing an electroencephalograph on his sleeping son, Armond. Aserinsky teamed with Professor Nathaniel Kleitman, of the University of Chicago, and in 1957 they realised that the REM occurred only while the person was dreaming. This defined sleep into two different observable states, REM sleep, and NREM (non rapid eye movement) sleep.

In REM sleep we experience the classic dream, with its full imagery, feelings and apparent reality. In NREM sleep we do not dream in imagery, but have long trains of thought with little imagery. The brain is not idle at that time.

While you dream in REM sleep there are other differences, too. Your senses shut down. Even your ability to feel your limbs and body disappears. More radical still, during the REM period of dreaming, nerve impulses to your voluntary muscles are switched off, paralysing voluntary movements, except for your eyeballs. This amazing change is thought to have developed in our distant ancestors because while dreaming the brain produces all the nerve impulses connected with the movements we make in our dream activity. If these impulses were not blocked, you would be walking, running or fighting while you dreamt.

If you take a moment to consider what this means, many dreams and sleep experiences will become understandable. Usually when you sleep and dream you are 'unconscious'. You have either completely or partly lost your ability critically to evaluate what is happening, and the action of dreams is largely unwilled or spontaneous. But suppose, as occasionally happens, you maintain some degree of critical awareness as you fall asleep, what would it be like? What would it feel like if you remained awake as you entered the process of sleep and dreams as did Tart's Miss Z? What would it feel like to become suddenly paralysed or without any awareness of your body?

Lots of people have done this so there is no need to guess. Firstly, your body and brain slow down and the breathing rhythm changes. Then, often quite suddenly, your sense impressions switch off. It is as if the 'volume' of your hearing, feeling and even your brain activity is suddenly turned right down or off. This is experienced as a disappearance of your body. With no experience of weight or limbs, you feel as if you are a floating awareness in a vast space, or that you are floating or flying in space. No wonder Janice and Mrs Jones were frightened. They had remained awake while asleep and met an experience of which they had no understanding.

This is still not the experience of dreaming, but one of a totally different way of being. It is like entering a different world with different rules. That is why it is sometimes depicted as entering a cavern, an 'underworld', or even a heaven-world. Some people feel as if they are dying when they remain awake and enter sleep. Perhaps that is why Carl Jung used the picture of an Egyptian tomb to depict the experience. It is this stage that gives rise to the impression of floating out of the body to those people who maintain partial awareness. This is why Mandy felt afraid, Janice was paralysed and Tart's Miss Z floated out of her body. As already explained, the EEG machine showed she was both awake and asleep.

Dreams — Doorway Beyond Self
While you dream your body is paralysed. But to some extent your will is also paralysed. Because of this Mandy felt the 'force' was pulling her along, even though she was saying 'No!' This is important to remember if you are to understand and work with dreams. If you hold your breath for any length of time an enormous pressure to continue breathing builds up until it overcomes your will. You can accept the compulsion to breathe as normal because you have grown up with the continuous act of breathing. But supposing some force, like the drive to breathe, took control of your body, emotions and mind, and pushed you toward movements and feelings you had not willed. You might feel very threatened. You might believe that an alien force was controlling you. You could be terrified you were going mad. Something apparently other than your own will would be gripping you.

Freud said that dreams are 'ego alien'. He meant that when you sleep, your waking personality is involved in a drama that you have not willed. You simply witness or experience the dream, often without choice. Sometimes you might wish to escape from it, which is a spontaneous and unexpected experience. It occurs in sleep when your conscious self is relaxed and in a condition in which it allows the unexpected to happen. In the case of a dream, this means permitting a drama to unfold, allowing strong emotions, physical movements, sexual feelings and speech other than from your conscious will. Truly, something other than what you usually consider to be your 'self' is controlling you.

If this happened while you were awake — something taking hold of your body and either paralysing it or making it dance — you might be terrified. Realising this, now look back on Janice and Mrs Jones's description of their dreams. Also, think about the experience of nightmares where the process of self-regulation is attempting to work on unfinished business, but you feel it as something terrifying. However, remember that it is not an evil force gripping you: it is your own process of life trying to heal and grow you. It is your own will, but from your inner life rather than your waking personality.

Of course, this exposure to a conscious descent into the world of sleep and dreams does not happen to all of us. It is nevertheless important to grasp the message clearly that dreams arise from a source other than your conscious will. Your own decisions and preferences may interact with the process just as they do so with your drive to breathe. It is necessary to understand that dreams are, like breathing, a powerful process of self-regulation. Because massive interference with your breathing is life-threatening, the self-regulatory process overcomes your will quickly in order to keep your being balanced and healthy.

Similarly, your conscious choices about what emotions you allow, what sexual feelings you permit, and what direction in life you take may well hold back important parts of your nature or growth. To keep balance, dreams might forcefully intrude just as the urge to breathe does. But as the danger is not so immediate, your dreams only nudge you toward completing unfinished emotional and sexual business.

The immense importance of this in our psychological and physical health can be grasped by the following examples:

a) In 1959, psychologists closely monitored Peter Tripp, a New York disc jockey, as he stayed awake for 201 hours. After four days, he had trouble recalling the alphabet.[10] Hallucinations and paranoia quickly followed. The drive to dream became compulsive to the point where hallucinatory images blanked out his vision of the 'real' world. Experiments to deprive people of their dreams, other than that with Peter Tripp, had to be stopped because of this compulsion to dream.[11]
b) Research with animals depriving them of sleep or dreams, in which the tests did not have to be stopped, ended in their deaths within twenty-one days.

We can gather from this that stopping breathing can kill you quicker, but dreams are also vital to your well-being. They are part and parcel of your self-regulatory process. Understanding and working with them can aid how your conscious personality relates to the life-giving processes within you. Just as you can stifle a yawn, suppress perspiration, hold back a sneeze, tense against trembling and inhibit crying and anger — all of which are self-regulatory processes — so you can suppress self-regulation in your dreams. Interference decreases your power to heal and be fully alive. Working with dreams increases the efficiency of self-regulation and therefore enhances your life.

What Are You On?
2. The process that causes us to dream creates fantastically realistic hallucinations.

My son Leon told me a dream that shows how persuasively they can lead us to believe we are experiencing objective reality.

> I was awake in bed with my eyes closed, realising the alarm had not gone off, so I could remain in bed. Just to be safe, I opened my eyes and looked at my watch. It showed seven, so I still had another half-hour. Just as I was looking at my watch, I heard a friend who lives in the same house calling me, saying it was late. I then realised I was dreaming, forced my eyes open and looked at my watch. It was nearly eight.

Not only are we convinced in the dream that what we witness is objectively real, but the dream process can also sometimes function while we are awake. When this happens, unless we are well aware of the process, very strange conclusions might arise concerning what is going on. Les, a friend, often experienced such waking dreams. One example is that while guests were staying at his house, Les slept in his daughter's room. He woke in the morning to see a very small man, about three feet tall, walk out of his daughter's cupboard. Feeling angry that anyone should be hiding in her room, he jumped out of bed and chased the man down the stairs. It was not until he was nearly at the bottom of the stairs that the man disappeared and Les realised he had been 'dreaming'.

This waking dream process is most likely the cause behind many experiences of alien abduction or seeing ghosts. Nevertheless, we should not immediately say such events are therefore 'all in the mind'. Do not forget that what Miss Z saw in her sleeping/waking dream turned out to be objectively real. Even when this is not the case, after thirty years of exploring the associations and feelings behind dream images, I still see that even the most bizarre of dreams or waking dreams arise out of the unique dynamics of your own body and mind. Therefore, a dream can reveal what has been obscure or even hidden about you.

The everyday relevance of this is that when you come to consider a dream, you may be tempted to view the characters or places in it as somehow unconnected to yourself. Dreaming about your mother or your partner, you might think, 'What does this say about them?' rather than 'What does this say about me?' Having helped thousands of people explore their dreams, I know just how deep the habit is to treat all dream characters and places as something apart from yourself. Dreams depict your fears and longings as exterior people, animals, places and things. Your sexual drive may be shown as your friend Jane, who is always talking about her love life. Fears you have can be given the shape of a fierce dog or a shadowy figure lurking outside your house. Your ambition might be portrayed as your boss at work, your changing emotions as the sea or a river, while the present relationship you have with your ambition could be expressed in the events or plot of the dream.

If this can be grasped, you have taken a great step toward gaining treasures from your dreams. You have made an even greater step in accepting more responsibility for your mind and emotions instead of blaming your feelings on someone else. But why should you have these visions of the night? Why should these nocturnal visions sometimes invade the day? Why should you dream at all? The answers to these questions have probably already been given. But they are so important it is worth looking at them again, perhaps from a fresh angle.

Some modern dream theories suggest that during sleep the brain produces random impulses that are possibly put into some sort of order by inbuilt desires to place meaning on experience. This proposes that dreams just happen as a by-product of brain activity and are not vitally important. It strikes me, and other professionals who have worked with dreams for years, that these theorists disregard vast amounts of evidence, such as continuously recurring dreams, dream themes and out-of-body experiences, in order to make their theory seem plausible.

Most of us can experience for ourselves that our body has a very powerful integrity. By this, I mean you have inbuilt processes that protect your body against attack from bacteria and viruses. Your body's functions and organs work together, forming a unique entity. You have processes that pushed your growth onward at a certain age, and contained its progress at another. Your body has a very definite purpose — to survive.

This purpose, this identity and drive, is one of the great features of your body and its processes. The wonder of how billions of cells work together is still a mystery being explored by scientists. Yet when it comes to mental function this view is somehow lost or rejected. Are the development, growth and survival of your psychological identity any less fought for than physical survival? Of course they are not. The enormous psychological and emotional defences, and the many processes of mind that are clearly observable, all confirm it.

In his book *Dreams and Nightmares*, Dr J. A. Hadfield describes this purposeful process clearly:

> If a branch of a tree is cut, new shoots spring out; if you injure your hand, all the forces of the blood are mobilised until that wound is healed and you are made whole. It is a law of nature. So it is psychologically: every individual has potentialities in their nature, all of which are not merely seeking their own individual ends, but each and all of which

serve the functions of the personality as a whole. Our personality as a whole, like every organism, is working towards its own fulfilment.

Dr Hadfield connects this even more directly with the overall self-regulatory physical processes in saying:

> There is in the psyche an automatic movement toward readjustment, towards an equilibrium, toward a restoration of the balance of your personality. This automatic adaptation of the organism is one of the main functions of the dream as indeed it is of bodily functions and of the personality as a whole.

You dream because your psyche wishes to establish its own well-being, growth and fulfilment as urgently as your body seeks to breathe and your heart strives to beat. Enquiring into your dreams emphasises and aids this drive to exist — and exist well.

Language and Dreams

3. Dreams employ imagery in the same way your everyday language uses images to express what you feel and think. Dreams also reflect our thought processes.

If you put into a painting or dream sequence the many idioms or word images you commonly use, you would have thousands of ready-made images or sequences. To name but few: Cat on a hot tin roof — Fish out of water — Wolf in sheep's clothing — On the right scent — Feeling blue — Down-to-earth — In hot water — Thrown in the deep end — Up in the air — Out on the town — Underhanded — Eyes for you only.

Most of the words you use also have many meanings. 'Run', for instance, which appears at first sight to be a simple concept, has over forty definitions in *The Concise Oxford Dictionary*. We can run a race, a bath or a shop. Water can run, so can a nose, or a train on its tracks. Dreams depict all these subtle meanings and implications. But equally — or more important still — is the fact that dreams display your very personal feeling associations with people and objects. This is perhaps one of the most important points as far as understanding your own dreams is concerned; so looking at a couple of examples is useful.

A woman whom I once helped to explore her dream with a group I was leading told us a dream in which her daughter, Sarah, was at university, but was murdered. The woman, who I will call Alice, said her daughter was just starting university. It would be her first time away from home. Alice thought the dream was about Sarah, possibly a warning. However, as we helped Alice explore the dream, her associated feelings about her daughter were sheer terror that Sarah would be badly hurt or murdered when she left home. So Alice's dream was very straightforward and had put into dramatic form fears about her daughter, not presentiments about an objectively real Sarah.

Most of our dreams are like this. Dreaming of our car may very well depict the 'Dream Dictionary' definition of car — our ability to move around and make choices. But perhaps the vehicle is one in which you had an accident, so experienced a brush with death. Possibly it took you hard work and sacrifice to purchase. These special associations will certainly be connected with your dream car. The feelings behind the symbol may be intense, deeply influencing your decisions and responses.

Often we have not clarified or previously put into words what we feel about a person or object that suddenly arise in our dream. That is possibly why they appear as a symbol instead of a clear realisation. But another reason we dream in images and events is that an image, just like a trademark or a wedding ring, represents a whole spectrum of ideas, feelings, and memories. They are all integrated in that one image. It would take many words to express what one image conveys.

An interesting example of special associations and synthesis was sent to me while working for Teletext. It came from Elizabeth, of Nottinghamshire:

> I am twenty-three years old, and have been married for two years. Recently, I dreamt I was on holiday in Egypt with my husband and parents. We were in the desert. I saw sand dunes ahead and camels with two humps. One of the camels licked my face. Could you please tell me what it means?

Elizabeth was married, but had not been able to have children. The desert depicts how barren she feels. Because she is on holiday with her family, she is shown as feeling supported by her husband and parents. But they also represent marriage and the ability or expectation to have a child. Added to this, the camel with its two humps is used by Elizabeth to express her feelings about pregnancy — she wants two bumps herself by becoming pregnant twice. The camel is a survivor in barren places so the symbol is a hopeful communication between Elizabeth's unconscious wisdom and her doubts and fears.

Therefore, the camel synthesises many important feelings for Elizabeth: namely, her struggle to survive the feelings she has about being childless, positive feelings that she will become pregnant and her desire for two children.

Apart from language in images and direct associations, dreams also abstract our sense impressions as we do in thinking. For instance, many ideas are abstractions. Feelings like love, justice or loyalty are abstracted from deeds done by one or many people. Dreams tend to put such abstractions into concrete images. From such a process, much that appears mysterious in religion becomes more understandable. What would happen, for example, if we gave love or the mysterious process of life itself a human form?

Self-Monitoring
4. Dreams are in no way any less meaningful, no less an expression of your past, your totality or your human condition, than any other tiny, wonderful part of your life.

During a medical examination, you may have your pulse taken, and give blood and urine samples. From a small amount of both, a clever pathologist can tell you a great deal about your health. A brilliant pathologist could probably astound you with what he or she deduced about your health, and even your personal history. Each tiny part of you holds in it something of your whole being. Fortunately, we have the physical evidence of holograms to illustrate this. When a piece of film containing a holographic image is cut in half, each half still reproduces the whole image. More amazing is that even when the film is halved again and again, each small part contains the whole image.[12]

When thoroughly investigated, dreams have within them the essence of your whole life. That is not said out of an attempt to make them seem mysterious. Having helped people discover insight into dreams they experienced up to eighteen years previously, I realised that an old dream held within it powerful attitudes that were the shaping influences in the current personality. It was akin to looking at the part of a tree's trunk that had been formed many years before and seeing how the current tree emerged. Not only were such dreams indicators of what had gone before, but the templates of what was to come.

More important still in understanding what a dream may be is to realise that most of us have a very out-of-date view of what our brain is, or even what our physical body is. New evidence arising from quantum physics and neurophysiology suggests that our body and brain, like a holographic image, are a projection from an entirely different dimension. To quote Michael Talbot, author of *Holographic Universe*:

> ... there is evidence to suggest that our world and everything in it — from snowflakes to maple trees, to falling stars and spinning electrons — are ghostly images, projections from a level of reality so beyond our own it is literally beyond both space and time.[13]

The main proponents of this view are two of the world's leading thinkers, David Bohm, a University of London physicist, and Karl Pribram, a neurophysiologist at Stanford University. Bohm, a protégé of Einstein, arrived at a holographic view of the universe after years of dissatisfaction with the inability of older theories to explain many of the phenomena of quantum physics. Pribram's conviction arose because of neurophysiological puzzles he encountered. For example, people who have hearing in only one ear know the direction from which a sound comes even though they need the stereophonic impression from two ears to distinguish direction. Also, most of us can recognise the face of a friend we have not seen for years, even if he or she has changed enormously.[14]

No attempt will be made to argue this theory as our theme is understanding dreams, not exploring quantum physics and neurophysiology. It is mentioned because it is a theory that begins to give a cohesive view of the various phenomena of the universe and the human brain. In doing so, it shows how strange and previously scientifically rejected phenomena, such as prophetic dreams, verified out-of-body experiences, telekinesis and remarkable healing body transformations, can occur.

However, as far as the present argument is concerned, the importance of the theory is this: if dreams represent your whole being, if your body/brain/personality are a projection from a source beyond what you know as time and space, then your real self, your true being, is not what you generally accept. At base, you are not a creature influenced by the vagaries of the three-dimensional world with its ever-changing environment, its birth and death. You are not your body, although you experience its changes. You are not ultimately the heartaches and passions you experience, though you may identify with them deeply. All these are images on the screen of consciousness, not consciousness itself.

The quality of some dreams suggests they are an expression of your timeless self. They connect it with what you identify as your body and personality. They also link the source with what is projected into time and space. Like the operator of an underwater robot who looks through the lenses of the robot's eyes, you too may perspire, your heart race and your spirit feel defeat as the robot achieves its task, or is threatened or crushed by its environment.

Here is a dream I witnessed that might help demonstrate the possibilities of a timeless self. It happened to my first wife, Brenda, nearly thirty years ago. In her dream, Brenda was looking at the baby boy of two friends of ours — Su and Grant[15] — who lived hundreds of miles away. Just over a week before the dream, we received a short letter from them saying that Su had given birth to a baby boy. There was no other information. We did not have a telephone, so Brenda was certainly not in touch with Su and Grant other than by letter.

As Brenda watched the baby in the dream, she understood — or a voice from behind told her — that he was ill. She was given to understand that the illness from which he was suffering would necessitate taking a drug every day of his life to survive. This burden, Brenda was told, was because in a past life the personality born as the baby had committed suicide using a drug.

Brenda and I explored her dream as we believed it was something relevant to her emotions or life. We did not arrive at any insight. Just in case the dream had meanings we didn't understand, I sent a letter to Grant and Su describing the dream. Some time later, we received a reply. It said they had been slightly worried about the baby before the letter arrived. He had not been feeding properly and was fretful, but the description of the dream crystallised their fears, so they took him to their doctor. The GP found nothing obviously wrong, but suggested further tests. Performed in hospital, they quickly revealed that the baby was dying. This was due to the lack of an enzyme necessary to the digestion of calcium. He had to be given a drug every day to compensate for this lack. That baby is now an adult man — and still has to take a daily tablet to stave off death.

From where did that dream come? Who is the dreamer? Do we dream only when we sleep and meet apparent fantasies of the night? Or are we dreaming when we identify completely with our 'waking' personality and all we experience in the drama of physical life? This is not a suggestion that physical life is unreal, only that our perception of it as an ultimate reality might be flawed. Witnessing Brenda's dream and the drama of Su's and Grant's child proved to me that what we know and believe consciously is only a tiny part of what is possible. It was a clue to what our real existence might be.

The Undying

Virtually every culture has a concept of an undying timeless or transcendent part of human life. Christianity names it Spirit. Buddhism calls it Buddha, a realisation of which all can experience. The Naskapi Indians see it as Mista'peo, meaning the Great Man or Great Being. In the Upanishads, Hinduism describes it as Atman. The name for it in Islam is Ruh.

Maria von Franz, principle disciple of the psychiatrist Carl Jung, says, 'Mista'peo dwells in the heart and is immortal; in the moment of death, or shortly before, he leaves the individual, and later reincarnates himself in another being.'[16] The Naskapi Indians attempt to listen to the counsel of Mista'peo through their dreams. They believe this internal Great Being helps them in practical and moral ways, just as Brenda was advised in her dream about the illness of Su's baby.

The Hindus describe Atman as the part of us untouched by the variations of time and circumstance. Nevertheless, the Atman is trapped in our perception of the constantly changing world of our everyday experiences unless we wake up to what is happening.

THE TRANSCENDENT

In most great cultures, gaining experience of the transcendent is considered one of the greatest boons in life. The reason is that access to the transcendent brings many benefits, such as:

Release from limiting habits of thinking and relating, so enabling entry to enormous creativity.

Awareness of an eternal life not dependent upon the body.

A sense of your place in life, and therefore self-confidence and a view of what goals you want to achieve.

Contact with a power that is transforming, can heal physical illness and bring release from trauma and the burden of cultural and family negative influences.

Bohm's theory tries to bridge the gap between the science of holography, the hidden workings of the mind, the ancient mystical teachings and modern quantum physics. Put briefly, in observing electrons, it is seen that objects in space which appear to be separate are really connected units of an unbroken wholeness just as each cell in our body is necessary to the well being of the whole. The transcendent Spirit, Atman or Great Being is that aspect of us knowing itself as the eternal, unbroken wholeness. The transcendent is often represented in dreams by a big man or woman, a shining object or person, a square, a holy being or a talking wondrous animal. This is why Mista'peo is called Great Being.

There are many dreams that express a meeting with the transcendent self; here are two examples. The first was told me by Aaron:

> I dreamt I was lying in a cellar. I was myself, yet at the same time, I was my wife and another woman I loved. I was in labour, and after a time the baby was born. It was a boy, a wonderful child. The membrane covered part of its face and I pulled it away. The baby then began to breathe, and looked about, fully conscious and very alert. Then, to my wonder, it spoke the name of Jesus, and said, 'It is gone'.
>
> When asked what was gone, the beautiful baby replied, 'The other ego, where has it gone?' I seemed to know exactly what it meant. The baby had been part of the cosmic awareness, of God consciousness, and was now but a babe; and I said, 'The cosmic still exists within you, to become known as you grow'. I then carried the baby from the cellar upstairs, and knew it to be a holy and wonderful child.

This second dream is from Kevin.

> An angel came to me and explained that before we are born we are all angels and are without limitations. When we are born we take on a life of limitations in order to learn something important to us. Then when we die at the end of that life we return to being an angel. All the limitations of life then disappear again.

When we dream of the transcendent, we experience something of life, as Kevin's dream puts it, beyond limitations. We touch something that gives us a taste of the timeless and eternal.

3
Science v. Experience and Religion

With the passing of each century it is more difficult to sustain religious beliefs. One of the main reasons for that is the information we receive. This alters our view of the world and our place within it. It is important to have a grasp of this shifting process in order to gain a basic understanding of dreaming and dreams.

Is the Universe a Machine or Divine?
One of the enormous shifts in viewpoint that most of us can recognise, even if we disagree with it, is the change arising from the insights given to the world by Galileo Galilei, René Descartes, Isaac Newton, and, later, Charles Darwin. The picture they gave us of the world — in fact, the universe — was that of a great machine, like a huge clock, with all parts being visible and understandable. They defined a universe in which everything was explainable in material terms. Before this the universe was God-driven, and humans were central in the scheme of things. It was easy to be religious because the information available with which to think was mostly descriptive of a God-driven world full of mysteries.

Gary Zukav, author of *The Dancing Wu Li Masters*, says that Galileo and Newton '. . . attempted to place "man" at the centre of the stage, or at least back on the stage; to prove to him that he need not be a bystander in a world governed by unfathomable forces. It is perhaps the greatest irony of history that they accomplished just the opposite.'[17] In a universe that is a great machine and runs like 'clockwork',

---

SCIENCE AND DREAMS

REM accompanies dreaming. We dream in regular cycles throughout sleep. Our longest dreams occur at the end of sleeping.

The most ancient creature to exhibit REM sleep is the platypus. This suggests dreaming started 250 million years ago.

REM sleep is only observed in warm-blooded animals.

we can predict just where the world will be in a thousand years. Without this skill, the space programme would not have been possible. But this view gives the suggestion that all humans are cogs in a huge machine with only an illusion of freewill. 'The universe is a pre-recorded tape playing itself out in the only way that it can.'[18]

Although cultural standpoints differ enormously, this Newtonian, mechanistic view of the universe has grown stronger over the years since he proposed it. Whether or not we agree, we are immersed in this world-view to a large extent. It pervades the very way we experience the world and ourselves. It shapes our world as most of the mechanical and electronic artefacts around us have arisen from it. It definitely moulds our attitudes to dreams and dreaming.

But since 1900, when Max Planck published his quantum theory, another great shift began. Quantum mechanics points out that the underlying stuff of the universe, subatomic particles, do not behave in a mechanistic way. Repeated experiments show that we cannot predict the behaviour of these particles. Not only that, but our observation of them produces changes. Gary Zukav writes: 'Philosophically the implications of quantum mechanics are psychedelic. Not only do we influence our reality, but, in some degree, we actually create it!'[19]

The New World View

To sum up, the old physics says that:
- There are immutable laws of nature which, once known, can be used to predict future events i.e. the movements of the moon.

SCIENCE AND DREAMS

The reason we do not act out our dreams is that a centre in the brain switches off muscle-activating signals. In animals in which this centre was deactivated, they were observed to live their dreams in fighting and hunting. This suggests dreams are a way of practising survival skills.

REM sleep appears to be essential. Humans deprived of it become irritable and anxious.

A few neuroscientists say that dreams are meaningless products of brain activity while we sleep. But most researchers reject this view. Dreams have too clear a narrative and coherence to be random. The

- The laws of nature are exterior to our own will and we cannot change them. King Canute could not stop the tide.
- The future is pre-determined by what went before, like a wound-up clock.
- Humans are small cogs in the giant machine.

The new physics says that:
- The behaviour of particles cannot be predicted. You can only estimate probabilities.
- Sub-atomic particles are influenced by the person observing them. In some degree, the observer actually creates what is observed.
- There is no such thing as objectivity. You cannot eliminate yourself from the universe. It and you are not separate. Everybody and everything has a standpoint within it and, therefore, a point of view.
- We are participators. The universe in some strange way may be brought into being by our participation.

Am I the Creator of My Own Life?

This long preamble is vital because the experience you face in waking life is extraordinarily like the old physics. You probably feel the world is solid and unchangeable, and that illness and events are brought about largely by external factors. The physical world may appear real and external to you.

The world you face in dreams is extraordinarily like the new physics. The environment — and even the people — are created out of your own conscious and unconscious desires, fears and thoughts. Each

---

majority of investigators maintain that dreams are a separate reality, playing a vital part in our health and waking life.

During many years' research, Dr Stanley Krippner produced statistical evidence suggesting we can be telepathic during dreams.

Using methods of analysing brain activity, various researchers — Dr Pierre Maquet at the University of Liege, for instance — have produced results pointing to the possibility that dreaming involves memory processing. Years before brain-scans gave us insight into brain activity, the well-known scientist Dr Christopher Evans said that dreams were a way of integrating new experience and learning from it.

change in attitude alters the situation you meet. Your dream world and you are one and the same. There is no separation. Each dream depicts a viewpoint. But each viewpoint is not a final reality. Rather it is an expression of infinite possibilities, even paradoxical opposites.

What this implies is that you are the creator of your own life, the author of your own life story. Here is a very graphic dream illustrating this. Tom told me:

> I was in a large prison cell with three other men. The dream seemed to cover a very long period of time, and we were never allowed out of the cell. We ate, slept, lived and defecated in the one room. At first, I was consumed with anger against everything and everybody who had put me in that cell. I would stand glaring out between the bars. Gradually, I realised that all my anger was completely ineffective. The only person who was hurt or ill at ease because of it was me, so I stopped being angry. After that, it became obvious that I was also the only sufferer of my other difficult feelings, such as that of being trapped or unsatisfied without activity. I dropped these, too, and they felt like old ghosts melting away, no longer haunting me.
>
> One day as I sat on my mattress, I felt the last 'ghost' drop away. Everything, even my jailers, were forgiven. It felt like a plug or block had fallen away inside me. A great torrent of joy rushed up within me, filling me, pouring out of me. So great was this pleasure that I cried out involuntarily, and felt my face was shining as if alight with something beyond my old, small self. My cell-mates were disturbed by the powerful feelings radiating from me and called the jailers. They all stood at the cell door staring at me while I sat motionless and radiating. I knew that nothing could ever be the same again. I was completely free, even though I remained in the cell. What burst out of me had entered into each of the other men. They were changed, too.

In dreams, we discover a world almost completely of our own making. We might exist in a hell of pain and fear, or feelings of being trapped. Conversely, we may live in a heaven of joy, such as Tom experienced. What Tom's dream demonstrates is that hell can become heaven by changing attitudes. In his dream, Tom took charge of feelings instead of continuing to blame them on everyone else or on his situation. His dream world then transformed. His transformation was also brought about because he experienced his transcendent self, influencing his waking life for years to come. It helped Tom to see that his view of the world was largely of his own making. By dropping the 'ghosts' of his resentments and blaming, he could find peace and joy now, not in some future heaven.

Is your waking life so different? You may also be trapped in attitudes and emotions, fears and uncertainties. You might be imprisoned by a mental climate or mental world that are invisible, intangible and often not recognised. Nevertheless, such attitudes are equally as imprisoning as living on Devil's Island, or existing in the past like a slave. They are just as real, equally as awful.

However, there is one difference between the dream and the waking world. In the latter, we share a 'dream' or a created environment with millions of others. If you look around at your surroundings in the so-called real world of waking, they are created by thoughts and emotions, by illusions or pain, as they are in a dream. How many towns have been built by the greed of speculators? How many schools are impoverished because the priorities of the community are that a factory or race-course are more important than a rich environment for their children? How much of the world's beauty is destroyed because we create a hell instead of a heaven? We all live in a mutually created world of our own thoughts and feelings. We are all co-creators of our world. We are the almost sole creators of our personal dream world. We can change both if we wish.[20]

I am not going to suggest, like some dream writers, that your life will be transformed quickly by a few tricks with dreams, by visualising nice things, having sex with dream lovers or flying in lucid dreams. Your life is a great stream of events woven around very powerful themes of feelings and responses that give direction to what you do. Your life is a present expression of ancient events and themes in an attempt to work out the tapestry of the past. To transform your life is an amazingly creative and artistic process. It takes time. It takes courage. It takes your love. Meeting your dreams more fully gives new life. It brings a meeting with you the baby, you the adolescent, you the disabled and you the angel. You experience the transcendent. It transforms not only your life, but the world around you, too. But like Tom in his dream of imprisonment, you will have to stop blaming others or life for your difficulties; you will need to be honest and start observing who you are.

Time Line of Dreams

Before the sleep laboratories of this century there are no signs at all within past cultural knowledge that rapid eye movements accompanied dreaming. Of course, many people observed animals and humans while asleep and noticed the twitching of limbs and eyes. This had been recognised as connected with dreams. For instance, the Roman poet Lucretius of the first century BC watched a hunting dog twitch as it lay sleeping and concluded that the animal was chasing phantom prey in its mind. But the acute knowledge of REM sleep, of the clear-cut cycles of brain activity while sleeping and dreaming, had not been formulated. Often these different approaches and the information arising from them are presented as being hugely at variance. Looked at unsympathetically, this is certainly true. Even looked at sympathetically some statements about dreams can be seen as having little or nothing to do with what can be observed about dreaming.

An example is the tradition of dream interpretation that flourished in the sixteenth and seventeenth centuries and is unfortunately still seen today in titles such as Gustavus Hindman Miller's dream dictionary and Raphael's *Royal Book of Dreams*. About such books, Norman MacKenzie writes: 'Cheaply printed pamphlets or chapbooks were widely circulated in London at this period; they had such florid titles as *The Old Egyptian Fortune-Teller's Last Legacy*, The *Royal Dream Book*, *The Golden Dreamer*, and *A Groatsworth of Wit for a Penny*. Most of these were 24-page books, a few having coloured frontispieces.'[21]

An example from such books reads: 'To dream of knives is unpropitious; it betokens law-suits, poverty, disgrace . . . shows your sweetheart to be of a bad temper, and unfaithful, and that if you marry, you will live in enmity and misery.'

As MacKenzie says of such a dream book, it represents '. . . the most degenerate form of what was once regarded as a divine art; it lacks any real religious or magical sanction, and is simply an expression of popular superstition, like the belief in lucky numbers, lucky colours or birthstones. Whatever meaning may once have lain behind the symbols and the interpretation has long been lost.'[22]

Despite these few bad examples, the history of human dream knowledge is one full of emerging insight. Nevertheless, it is only when we place some ancient insights against the latest views of the new physics that we can achieve the sympathetic view mentioned. In his study of African tribal traditions, Adrian Boshier tells us that the *dingaka* — seers or diviners — of the tribe get their results either through entering a trance state or from a dream.[23] The *dingaka* were — and still are — a practical part of tribal life. They are able to find lost objects or discover who committed a crime, and act as spiritual and psychological guides.

Looked at from the Newtonian Physics point of view, this sounds very suspicious and improbable. If the mind is merely made up of atoms, what is there to discover except the material world and what we have perceived of it through our senses? However, considered from the standpoint of the New Physics, what we know as the physical world may be a 'projection from a level of reality so beyond our own it is literally beyond both space and time'. Our present science is able to demonstrate that the very sub-atomic particles that make up our body are constantly in touch with similar particles in the farthest reaches of space. Therefore, it does not seem remarkable that a man or woman might learn how to touch the transcendent and gain unusual knowledge.

PAST DREAM THEORIES

Most older cultures believed dreams were produced by a god or evil influences they named spirits.

Dreams were looked to for guidance in hunting, major decisions and finding herbal cures for illness.

Early psychological practices used dreams as ways of understanding a person's state of mind and direction of growth.

In Ancient Greece, special 'dream' temples were erected to use in the healing of illness.

Describing the beliefs of the Huron Indians, in 1649 Father Ragueneau, a Jesuit priest, said their divinity was the dream. They believed the soul had hidden desires that reveal themselves in dreams. If not expressed, they could cause illness or even death. This long preceded Freud's similar theory.

The modern scientific approach to dreams started in ancient Greece. Plato and Aristotle suggested that the faculties of nutrition, sensation and reason could all play their parts in the making of the dream.

Prehistory

An idea of attitudes to dreams prior to the written word can be gained from such sources as the work of Adrian Bouchier among African tribal people. He discovered evidence of traditions used today that had existed for at least a million years in Africa. His findings suggest that dreams were seen as a means of entering a different state of mind in which things not possible in waking life could be achieved. These included gaining special knowledge of herbs and medicines, being warned of impending tribal or personal difficulties and as a means of initiation and seeing into the life beyond death. Initiation — an important part of life for most tribal people — was fundamentally about achieving a fuller level of identity and maturity. In other words, moving from child to youth, youth to maturity, and maturity to finding a personal relationship with the tribe and with the transcendent.

One of the frequent aspects of dream theory of ancient people is concerned with whether a dream was good or bad. Frequently, one finds mention of an evil or frightening dream. Many rituals were devised to deal with such dreams. Much of the work — and probably income — of priests was connected with helping people to avoid the bad influence of dreams.

In attempting to understand this, we must remember that a different term — such as use of the words 'evil spirit' — does not necessarily make such thinking primitive or unsophisticated. Millions of gallons of alcohol are consumed daily in the modern world to help deal with 'evil spirits'. In our language, we call these evil spirits despair, fear, depression and anxiety. Tons of tobacco are smoked daily for the same reason. Like us, ancient people needed ways of dealing with fear and anxiety. Whether it is through a priest or psychiatrist, there is a human need to keep one's psyche in health. That these despairing or anxious feelings were called 'spirits' does not make any difference to what was actually being dealt with.

Early History

The oldest possible writing is thought to be pictographs found in Henan province, China.[24] Written records concerning dreams date as far back as 4000 years. They are from ancient Egypt and contain many references to dreams. The biblical stories of Joseph and

Pharaoh give us a clear picture of how dreams were thought to represent important matters at that period. Dreaming of seven thin and seven fat cattle, Pharaoh immediately sought interpretation. He realised even then that the dream used symbols.

The written records available of this ancient approach to dreams are a derivative of a much older oral tradition such as shown in the African culture. The Chester Beatty papyrus contains 200 accounts of dreams, and dates from about 2000 BC. These writings took up themes from even older documents. The oldest known library is that of Nineveh, dating from 5000 BC. This contained the Ashurbanipal dream book. Many modern dream dictionaries gained their inspiration from this. For instance, the Ashurbanipal tablets say that if a man flies repeatedly in his dreams, whatever he owns will be lost. *Zolar's Encyclopaedia and Dictionary of Dreams*, published in 1963, repeats this by saying, 'Flying at a low altitude: ruin is ahead for you.'

The Egyptians believed that from dreams they gained 'warnings, advice, success in love or other ventures, recovery from illness or merely pleasurable experiences'.[25] Many modern ideas about dreams owe their origin to ancient dream books written at the time. For example, contraries in dreams are often used: dream of death and it means a long life. The idea of 'good' and 'bad' dreams arises again and again, with such books as Raphael's using this approach throughout. It is an obvious way to defer anxiety about the dream rather than understand it.

The Egyptian interpretations took account of verbal puns, asso-

---

PHARAOH'S DREAMS

'And Pharaoh said unto Joseph, I have dreamed a dream, and there is none that can interpret it: and I have heard say of thee, that thou canst understand a dream to interpret it.

'And Joseph answered Pharaoh, saying, It is not in me: God shall give Pharaoh an answer of peace' — Genesis 41.15.

EGYPTIAN DREAMS

'In a dream — as well as in a vision at dawn — was shown a man surpassing in size, of glorious form, beautifully clad.' Here the transcendent is depicted as a great man.

An inscription in front of the giant sphinx at Giza describes the dream of King Thutmose IV. The god Hormakhu appeared and promised him the kingdom if he would clear the sands away from the sphinx.

ciation of ideas and common cultural idioms long before Sigmund Freud wrote about them. Their ideas influenced many later cultures. But the Egyptians had been similarly influenced in their turn, probably by the Assyrians. What may be original with the Egyptians is the cult of dream incubation. In this approach, the dreamer seeks a dream as a means of help or healing, perhaps by using a ritual or prayer.

Pre-Christian and Christian
The Christian approach to dreams arose originally from the Jewish religion and the writings in the Old Testament. The dream of Pharaoh is an example of the long-established tradition among the Hebrews to interpret dreams. Many dreams in the Old Testament are introduced with such phrases as 'And God said unto him in a dream'[26] or 'But God came to Abimelech in a dream by night, and said to him'.[27] It is clear that being a nation with a conviction of a single God, Jews believed important dreams were messages from Him. Also, as Joseph's words of interpretation suggest, the correct translation was divinely inspired or given.

If we put this into more general language, we can say that dreams were thought to originate from a source beyond one's limited physical senses. The understanding of a dream could be found through opening to one's intuition rather than from defined logical thinking. However, as with many cultural traditions there were precedents upon which dreams were judged and interpretations arrived at. For instance, the Talmud suggests rules for interpreting dreams. As with any people trying to maintain their identity, the Jewish aim for interpretation was partly to bring individual and group cohesiveness. In Deuteronomy 13.1 a warning is given about prophets receiving false messages in dreams. If the dream in any way suggests worshipping another god, '. . . that dreamer of dreams, shall be put to death; because he hath spoken to turn you away from the Lord, your God.'

The penalty of death for a dream gives us a clue to an aspect we should not overlook. This can be highlighted by the story of God causing Adam to fall into a deep sleep (see Genesis 2.21), when God works His will on him.[28] This idea of sleep and dreams having the possibility of your mind and experience being directed by another will — the Divine will — lies at the root of the way dreams were considered in the Bible. Adam's sleep has to do with identity. During his sleep, something was taken out of Adam — Eve/Aisha — that had its own existence from him, and which led to an awareness separated from God. This story is about the emerging of a personal will, a will that did not, as in the Garden of Eden, have to be entirely that of God.

This is an extraordinary story if we stand aside from any dogma or our negative associations with religious terms that might obscure our view. It is an account of how Christianity came to develop a personal will and not simply follow the group or be dominated by internal instincts. The Bible also tells us that non-conformity might be punishable by death. The Christian relationship with dreams has an internal struggle between the individual will and the will of God — or at least, the will of the community.

Sigmund Freud

Much of what is presently attributed to Freud was put forward by earlier thinkers and writers. Symbolism in dreams was recognised before the Pharaohs. Hidden desires expressed in dreams were described by the Huron Indians. The concept of the unconscious is also suggested by such hidden desires. What Freud did give us was his technique of exploring dreams through their symbolism and content. He also unveiled the enormous influence of early sexuality and trauma. The release of trauma had been witnessed and written about as early as Anton Mesmer. Freud was the figure who presented this in a way reasonably acceptable to the standards of the time.

Previously, there had been no systematic attempt to link a dream to very personal associations with the symbols. Freud gave us a geography of the mind that became common language in such words as unconscious, the id, super-ego, repression, persona, Oedipus-complex and so on. Along with Breuer, Freud pointed out how some

FREUD DESCRIBED DREAMS AS:

- 'Thoughts in pictures'. Early writing systems are the same, like hieroglyphics.
- 'Ego alien'.
- 'Hallucinatory'.
- 'Drama'. Most of our dreams have definite plots, with a beginning, middle and end.
- Dreams, he said, have different 'moral standards', and enjoy access to a more active 'association of ideas'. Thus, creativity or enhanced memory result.

neurotic behaviour was symbolically meaningful. It was an example of how the unconscious worked. For example, under conditions of stress a person might have an attack of asthma because he or she cannot 'breathe the atmosphere at home'. Another vomits because he or she can't 'digest' what is happening. In his work with individuals, Freud usually offered his own interpretation. His method of following associations did not stick to the dream.

Some of the most useful aspects of Freud's work to remember when exploring your own dreams are :

- The importance of the bonding between child and parents in creating life-long patterns of behaviour.
- The place such acts, as actual or perceived abandonment, and absence of expressed affection, have in creating trauma in the infant — trauma that creates life-long difficulties.
- Dreams are a way to become aware of what usually remains unconscious.
- Despite recent critics discounting Freud's evidence for infant sexuality, there is too much material for it to be rejected completely. What many people do is to look at their own experience and conclude that infant sexuality does not exist because they are unaware of it in their life. That was precisely Freud's point: it is unconscious.
- Psychic or inner reality is often very difficult to separate from external reality. Freud struggled with this in regard to women's experience of abuse.

A MAN IN HIS LATE TWENTIES DREAMT THIS AFTER READING AND REJECTING FREUD'S IDEA THAT BOYS DESIRED THEIR MOTHER

'I was in a dark and strange cul-de-sac. I groped to a door at the end of the cul-de-sac, and knocked on it.

'An elderly woman opened it. Without saying a word, I grabbed her and had sex with her. This awoke her passions, and she took me upstairs, as she had not had sex for twenty years. Her husband knocked at the door, but somehow she got rid of him for good. She then fell out of a window to her death.'

An elderly woman often represents your mother. The husband being 'got rid of' shows the boy's feelings of rivalry. The woman's death is also a part of the Oedipus story.

Carl Jung

Jung felt that human life is meaningful and has its roots in a transcendent reality. In this and other ways he differed from Freud, who was at first a collaborative colleague. Jung did not, as Freud, see the unconscious as a storehouse only of repressed infantile and unsocialised urges. It was a place of mystery and life. It included not only the widest storehouse of personal and family experience, but stretched beyond this, linking each of us with a collective experience of life. Jung said that this 'collective unconscious' holds within itself the merged experience of all that have lived.

Also from the unconscious arose what Jung called the influence of the Self. He defined the Self as the whole of a person. This is distinct from the narrow focus of Self we know in our daily life. For example, if you could have a sense of all your memories rather than simply what is relevant to the moment, you would hold a different view of all you did. Jung described this as similar to a ball with a small black circle drawn on it. The small black circle is our normal waking awareness whilst the ball is the Self.

From the Self — a more total awareness — arises what Jung called the 'transforming influence'. Our sense of wholeness, however unconscious it may be, leads us towards becoming more inclusive of our total potential. Jung taught that part of our wholeness is an awareness of being an intrinsic and unseparated part of the universe. Dreams are often an expression or a reflection of the Self. As such, they are self-regulatory and can lead to what Jung called 'individuation'. This is an attainment of your own personal identity beyond the sense of yourself you arrive at from such matters as class, role, gender, economic situation and physical appearance.

Jung was a psychiatrist working with and training a great number of people. A major emphasis of his work was on dreams. His approach was quite different to Freud. The major points are:

● The dream was seen as a source of information, not an attempt to disguise meaning, as Freud thought.

● Because he honoured the wisdom of the unconscious, Jung was intent on unfolding what the drama and structure of the dream held in it. He did not lead away from the dream with associations. However, he added his own insights to what the dreamer might discover.

- Jung encouraged people to explore a dream using active imagination, a way of honouring personal fantasy. He also suggested allowing the body to fantasise.[29] He wrote that fantasy is necessary because the conscious mind has no idea or experience of what is held within unconsciously. Not only might you find the pain of past trauma, but also what Jung called the 'dark possibilities', the unknown potential. You have to 'let go' of your consciously held convictions in order to allow the voice and experience of the unconscious speak, to permit more of yourself to be lived.
- To help people discover their associations with something in their dream, Jung would embrace the dream setting and format, not encourage associations that led away.
- If dreamers found difficulty in arriving at an association, Jung asked them to describe the symbol in their own words, as if he knew nothing about it. Therefore, if you dreamt of a table, you might say something like: 'It is an item of furniture usually made of wood and having four supports. Upon these, a flat surface is fixed so that you can place objects, food, books, etc. at a level nearer your hands or mouth.'
- Use of the term 'the Self' was Jung's way of bringing the transcendent dimension into his work. This was something Freud never did. Later, in methods like Psycho-Synthesis this approach to psychological growth and healing was extended, and is now frequently met under the name Trans-personal.

Alfred Adler

It was Adler who introduced the phrase 'inferiority complex' to the public and thus drew attention to this common phenomenon. Adler studied medicine and became a disciple of Freud, but diverged from him, as did Jung, over Freud's insistence that the sexual impulse was dominant. Adler's viewpoint was often summarised as 'the will to power'. This means that individuals stand between their own inner feelings and drives, and the influence of external society. Within these two worlds, an individual seeks to survive as best he or she can. Adler maintained that each of us develops our own personal style toward this survival. His psychotherapeutic work was aimed at helping the individual find this personal stance.

Adler viewed dreams as a window into a person's aggressive impulses and desire for fulfilment. He never used dreams as fully as

Freud or Jung, but believed they could help dreamers define two often conflicting aspects of their experience — their image or sense of themselves, and their sense of what is socially acceptable. Adler therefore felt that in our dreams we not only see what we think of ourselves and what our environmental situation is, but also find a definition of our techniques for satisfying the drive to deal with and succeed in the world. He called his approach Individual Psychology.

Adler did not see a great boundary between the conscious and unconscious personality. He felt that individuals could be observed to have the same attitudes and fears in dreams as they exhibited in waking life. From this standpoint, the dream is not something disconnected with your known personality, but a process which is attempting to add to or evolve your lifestyle. Therefore he did not, as Jung, believe the dream had a wealth of cultural or collective wisdom, or was an expression of a more complete self. For Adler, the dream was 'a tentative feeler toward the future', 'a dress-rehearsal for life', in which the dreamer reveals his hopes, fears, and plans for the future. But he did admit that in our dreams we are wiser than we know.

Adler gave generalised significance to themes arising in dreams. He described some of these as:

● Dreaming of *paralysis* arises from feeling hopeless about a problem confronting you, or believing it has no solution.
● Dreaming of *travelling* is an expression of your direction and progress in life.
● Dreaming of *falling* reflects fears about loss of face and falling in social favour. Adler said this was a theme often dreamt by neurotics.
● Dreaming of *flying* is a theme referring to problem-solving and positive confidence. It portrays the overcoming of obstacles, and occurs to people who are directing their lives to positive ends.
● Being *nude* in dreams expresses concern about being seen by others as having imperfections, or feeling your imperfections are exposed to view.
● Dreaming about people who are *dead* suggests the person is still influenced by that individual and has not become independent of him or her.
● The *roles* taken in dreams illustrate the style we adopt in waking life.

Fritz Perls

Fritz Perls was the main influence in an approach to dreamwork that was not interpretative. Unlike the Freudian or Jungian approach, which includes a lot of interpretative comment on the part of the analyst, Perls encouraged dreamers to explore and express their own response to each character and object in the dream. This was a complete break with tradition and the power of the 'expert' or authority figure as therapist. It developed a sense of personal ability and insight in the dreamer, enabling him or her to arrive at direct perception of how they had unconsciously formed their own dream. The insights into their own behaviour arising from this allowed someone more wisely to make decisions about action. It also opened a door of direct experience regarding the enormously potent content of an individual's dreams.

This approach was named Gestalt Therapy. It lends itself to peer dreamwork in which there is no external authority to judge the dreamer's insights or to tell them how to work. This has great benefits in that dream exploration can be undertaken by many people who cannot afford — or do not wish to undertake — psychoanalytic work. Its drawback is that dreamers may avoid their own resistances to uncovering deeper material, and conflicts or fears. However, in a good peer group this is not a problem if participants honestly attempt growth rather than mutual admiration.

> **DR ALAN RECHTSCHAFFEN, OF THE UNIVERSITY OF CHICAGO:**
>
> 'We think that sleep has an absolutely vital function because we sacrifice so much to it, meaning we don't protect our young, we don't gather food, we don't do all of the things that we don't have enough time to do when we're awake ... Sleep is so expensive that if it doesn't have a vital function, it's probably one of the greatest mistakes that evolution has ever made.'

The direct experience of your own dream which may arrive from Gestalt work is incredibly powerful and convincing. It gives insight into your own motivations and the ways in which you are influenced by your often unconscious past hurts and fears. This is very unlike the interpretative approach in which you mostly talk about the dream. From the platform of Perls's work a huge influx of people started finding personal growth and change through dreams.

Sandison — Grof — Ling and the Mind Laboratory

Many of us are quite well informed about the results of research in sleep laboratories. Most of us know what rapid eye movement sleep refers to. However, long before Kleitman and Aserinsky's discovery of REM sleep in 1953 and 1957, another huge area of research pertaining to dreams was being undertaken. This began in April 1943 when the Swiss chemist Albert Hofmann discovered LSD. Because of LSD's power to change states of consciousness, it was quickly experimented with in psychiatry.

One of the opportunities it offered was to observe unusual states of mind in an experimental way. This enabled psychiatrists and psychologists to study areas of mental and emotional functioning about which they had previously only theorised. Some of the main people involved were Sandison, Grof, Ling and Buckman.[30] Out of their work resulted an enormously expanded understanding of dreams, fantasy, levels of mental process and the unconscious. Unfortunately, the evidence of their observations is usually ignored by sleep laboratory research.

Although the findings from this source do not answer all the questions about the brain and human personality, something relevant to dreams is defined. It was seen from the research that there are at least two ways of 'thinking'. One avenue is to think with words and rational connection between associated ideas. This is the usual waking form of thought. Underlying this is thinking in images and linked similarities — what Tauber and Green called 'pre-logical thinking'.[31] This may be the way our ancient ancestors thought, not in words but in streaming fantasy or pictures that linked with feelings and past experience.

It is exactly this world of linked imagery, associations and emotions we enter in dreams. A problem that exists for us if we want to understand our dreams and extract the gold nuggets from them is that we usually attempt to understand this world of 'pre-logical' experience with our 'logical' thinking. We 'think' about our dream and attempt to interpret it according to our rules of logical thought. This is like trying to understand what it would be like to bathe in water by thinking about it when you had never been in water. Thinking will not come up with the answer.

Because of this McKenzie, author of *Dreams & Dreaming*, says: 'Under the influence of LSD a person can often interpret imagery — of a dream — that would seem meaningless in a state of normal consciousness.'[32] In fact, many people experienced spontaneous insight into their dreams while working with LSD. The insight was not simply a sort of intellectual knowing, but an ability to witness the intricate connections of past experience, feelings and imagery out of which a dream is woven.

One of the reasons this can occur is that LSD stimulates pre-logical thinking while at the same time allowing rational observation of what is experienced. Like Miss Z, the volunteers making the experiment could 'go to sleep' by entering the fantasy and pre-logical processes of dreaming and yet stay awake by maintaining a questioning mind. Therefore, the theories of Freud and the other great names could be checked against what people actually met in exploring their unconscious consciously. Dr Betty Grover Eisner, an American specialist in hallucinogenics, said of this:

> In the course of five years' work with the psycholytic or mind-changing drugs LSD, mescaline, psilocybin, ritalin and the amphetamines, one can only be awe-struck by the genius of Freud, Adler and Jung, and be saddened by the forces which split apart this trinity. Their observations and theories should be integrated; for the split skewed so many fundamental conceptions and discoveries.

W. V. Caldwell, who researched LSD use in clinics throughout the USA and Europe, echoes this: 'If the psychedelic experience had confirmed the theories of Freud, or Jung, or anybody else we might have been relieved. Instead, it has confirmed them all and added a few more besides.'[33] Caldwell is referring to the realisation that we all have a multi-storey brain/mind. Although the brain is composed of at least three levels, starting with the ancient brain stem, the medulla — similar to an ancient lizard brain — most of us are only aware of one level of experience. This is waking consciousness. Synthesising thousands of psychotherapeutic LSD sessions in clinics around the world, Caldwell gives a geography of these levels, listing them as four:

● Body-centred awareness that is deeply sensual. It is a level we all experience during infancy.

● The gestural. This emerges as we learn to express our feelings and needs through physical movement in infancy. Thus, we may expose our deepest hidden feelings in an unconscious body posture or movement. At this level, suppressed emotions manifest as psychosomatic pain or tension.

● The symbolic-mythic. This is a level seen in many older cultures where truths are expressed in the forms of myths and stories. We express our intuitions and needs through symbolic action as, when feeling trapped, we fight authority figures instead of having direct insight into our problem. We may act out what we feel, or what our life situation is, in a drama or play.

● The verbal-analytic. Here, we gain direct insight into situations and are able to verbalise them. We can define the symbol or myth.[34]

As adults we may, in fact, be living with a powerful body posture that we blame on tension when in reality it is an expression of deeply-felt experience. If we are unconscious of it, we are living only in our top-storey flat — the reasoning mind. What we can learn from this is that dreams often express these various levels of our mind in their drama or objects. Recognising them is a big step in becoming aware of how to understand the language of our dreams and to be whole. Consider some of these dream statements in connection with symbolic action: She is standing on a ledge ready to jump — I am standing with my husband — I reached out — I ran away — I hid in a closet — I could barely walk — He was walking along with his eyes closed — I was cold — I buried the body — I realised I had not fed the baby for whom I was caring — I was walking on ice.

Gayle Delaney — Robert van de Castle — Calvin Hall — Erich Fromm

Calvin Hall took a different approach to dreams than the laboratory technician or therapist. He collected thousands of dreams and analysed them for themes and content, using computer filing. He identified five major areas dreams dealt with. They are:

● Self-image. The roles you play or express in dreams indicate the image you have of yourself at the time.

● Image of other people. What other people are doing in your dreams indicates your feelings about them, and your relationship with them.

● View of the world. The environments you create in your dreams — ugly or beautiful — show how you feel about the world, whether it is inviting, threatening, a place of struggle, etc.

- Depiction of behaviour. What you do in your dreams shows your concepts and fears about what you can allow yourself to do, or the penalties for certain actions.
- Conflicts. Dreams often show what you struggle with. The difficult opposites of choice or behaviour are well depicted in many dreams.[35]

From his findings, Hall was sure that dreams were a much better indicator of a person's character and abilities than questionnaires. He paved the way for easy computer analysis using a series of dreams (see box). However, Hall was more than a statistical analyst.

> **COMPUTER DREAM ANALYSIS**
>
> By writing a journal of all your dreams, you can easily discover what are the main themes and images. A computer program such as *dtSearch*[36] quickly files everything you have written, meaning you can find common themes, characters, etc, in seconds. This often has startling results, for you discover such events as similar dreams at the same time of year — recurring themes — progress in your areas of difficulty.

Robert van de Castle became interested in Hall's work just after Castle received his PhD. While Castle was the subject in some of Hall's work with an encephalograph, Hall tried dream telepathy experiments, with obviously positive results.[37] This helped Castle to have an open mind about the transcendent aspect of dreaming, which he investigated more fully. But Castle explored dreams on a very wide front, and represents one of the best modern dream researchers and thinkers. By not taking on any one theoretical base, he has been able to see each approach as important.

This stance is also taken by Delaney, a psychologist who specialised in dream therapy. More than Hall and Castle, she has taken a stand against traditional roles of therapist and patient. Delaney pushes for what she states as 'the direct approach that does not need a therapist or detailed knowledge regarding the nature of dreams, and of the male and female psyche'. She has defined a method she calls 'dream interviewing'.[38] This will be looked at in a later chapter.

Erich Fromm is also worth mentioning because he is one of the psychiatrists who looked at the human situation from a different standpoint than Jung, Freud and many other psychologists. He saw the human condition not only as individual, but also largely a social one. He pointed out that many common human neuroses and anxieties arise from the historical development of social situations. Therefore, his books *The Forgotten Language* and *Escape From Freedom* are worth reading.

Summary

This very brief and limited look at the various approaches to dreams is nevertheless wide enough to show how vastly different are the theories. If some of the ideas are difficult to accept, there is no need for you struggle with them.

Scientific enquiries are not usually an attempt to undermine traditional views. They arise from an enormous inquisitiveness that, like the new physics, begins to re-evaluate the old traditions. The break with tradition provided by such people as Perls, Hall, Castle and Delaney have shown, if not in the laboratory then at least in human experience, that dreams are much wider than any theory. They are as multi-faceted and mysterious as human nature.

If you are going to approach them, you need to put hard theories aside and take curiosity into the relationship. If you walk the path with your dreams, be prepared to meet the sensual in yourself. Most of your encounters will be in the area of your own likes and dislikes, your fears and pains, your talents and weaknesses — in short your psychology. But be prepared to encounter the lover, the murderer, the small hurt child, the saint and the lunatic. They are all there in your dreams: they all play a role in your life.

Part of your wholeness is your body, mind and transcendent self. But each has many great rooms to explore. The mind alone has vast treasures of inherited wisdom passed to you non-verbally by parents and carers. You may doubt this just as in previous generations tales travellers told of elephants were doubted by non-travellers. Too many people have now explored their unconscious for us not to know some of the common inhabitants. If a scientist says he or she has explored dreams — in the laboratory and in thought — and cannot find any sign of the claims made by Jung and Freud, remember the difference in the story of the dip into water by the thinker and the swimmer.

Does your existence end when your body dies? Do you, as the dream about the sick baby destined to need a drug all its life suggests, already have a past from previous existences? Is the world as presented by your senses the real world, the truth? Or does the New Physics present the truth when it says we are part of an infinite universe and have a transcendent kernel beyond time and space? If that is a truth why is it you do not experience it? Are dreams a result of a wandering and disordered mind in sleep or a reflection of an awareness of your wholeness? Is there a fully formed eternal self or spirit at your base that teaches you through dreams and life? Or are you formed not from an eternal centre, but by life experience, body condition and culturation? Maybe there is not one truth, but many conflicting truths. If so, the only way is to find a way through the opposites and resolve the paradox.

Meanwhile, if you can simply say that you do not know what the truth is, this will leave you open to discover the possibilities in your dreams. It avoids the stalemate caused either by believing dreams are divine guidance — the whole truth — or that they are muddled images without worth. It lets in something of the possibility of which the New Physics speak when it says we are co-creators. Maybe this means you are not all-powerful. But neither are you powerless flotsam in a meaningless universe.

4
Travels in Virtual Reality

First Steps into Your Dreams
In this chapter, we are going to 'walk into your dreams' as if they are real places you can enter and explore. Although this may be a new idea for you, it is literally true. You can open a door and walk into your dream, discovering a new world of experience. It is an exciting world because when you walk into a dream, whether your own or someone else's, you get under the surface of yourself and other people. Real understanding comes because you are in the place where everything has meaning and speaks to you just as books do, and tell their story if you can read. The previous chapters laid the foundations. Now begin to build on them.

Remembering Dreams
Remembering a dream is, of course, the very first step. Some people can easily recollect several dreams a night while others hardly ever recall a dream. If you are among the latter, you need to realise that all of us dream for long periods each night so it isn't that you are not dreaming. There is no such thing as the 'night of dreamless sleep' you read about in fiction.

Sleep laboratories revealed that our dreaming periods are not haphazard. They arise almost with the regularity of a clock, so after around ninety minutes of sleeping you dream for a period of about five minutes. Then you sleep without REM dreaming for roughly another sixty minutes before you dream again for approximately nineteen minutes. From then on there are lengthening periods of dreaming, ending in a long period of dreams just before you wake from a night's sleep. Therefore, the most radical method of remembering a dream is to set a gentle alarm to wake yourself about an hour before your normal time.

If you are going to use this method, it is helpful to want to remember a dream and not to resent the waking. Hopefully, you can drop off to sleep again once you have recorded your dream. One of the easiest ways of making a record of your dream is to have a small tape-recorder under your pillow or near at hand, and speak your dream into it, otherwise you will need to rouse yourself enough to write the dream down. Do not wake and think you can remember your dream without recording it in some way. Dreams are often like snowflakes. You may have them in your hand, but they melt and disappear as you watch. Once gone, they are very difficult to recall.

An advantage of the tape recorder over the written record is that the latter is often very brief and details may be forgotten. With a tape recorder, you can remain half asleep and speak the whole dream. It does not matter if you remember 'only a fragment'. Do *not* discount what you recall because it is small. Like a holograph, fragments lead us into the whole.

A less radical way of remembering dreams is to become as interested as possible in what your dreams might be. This has proved effective in many cases. Your interest stimulates memory. The deeper level of your mind — the 'unconscious' — is as intelligent and 'human' as you are. It responds to interest, to love, to being listened to.

It is important with this method to wake up with care. What I mean by this is that even while awake, if you are thinking of something and your attention is attracted elsewhere, you may forget what you were thinking. Moving your body or opening your eyes when you awake allows an enormous influx of new impressions to blast away dream memories. Lie still, letting your attention drift backwards into the darkness of sleep. Then catch a dream by relaxing the tense expectations of your mind. Remembering anything requires a very special state of mind. Holding a fixed idea will often block memory. Drift, allow fantasy and hang loose. The dream will then materialise as if 'beamed-up' in an episode of *Star Trek*.

Sometimes blockages to remembrance of dreams are partly physical. Some people have a very concrete sort of personality. They do not fantasise much or have a wide range of emotional movement. This makes it less easy to remember dreams. Just as physical flexibility allows us to get into spaces an inflexible person could not, so flexible minds can reach dreams more easily. If you are taking the B range of vitamins, this may also act as a wall against dream memory. Lastly, a subtle block might be that you are shutting out a part of your own nature, your wholeness. You could be missing some element of yourself necessary for completeness. Admitting the possibility of such incompleteness is an important step in remembering dreams.

The Dream Journal
A dream journal is a wonderful item to create. When you gather many of your dreams and look back, especially if you have discovered insight into them, you will see the extraordinary story of yourself. You have amazing depths and heights only dreams permit you to see. You also have talents and a history so full of drama and interest that TV and films cannot compare.

If you have a computer, start a new file just for your dreams. If not, buy a special and thick book in which to record your dreams. When you remember a dream, put in the date and describe the dream as fully as possible. Do not write short notes. Doing so deprives yourself of the special information only you have. Some people give each dream a specific name to make it memorable. For instance, I experienced a dream where I had to give my name at an hotel reception. The receptionist asked me why I had a different name to last time. This dream could be called 'Problem Names'.

Along with the dream, write in any associations you may have with the people or places. This should include events the previous day that are similar or possibly triggered the dream as well as associations. An example is that you might dream of a particular coat, and you associate it with happy memories of being with someone you loved. Also, write in with as much detail as possible any insights you gain on the dream from later dreamwork. If you are putting your dreams on to a computer, electronically file the dreams with a programme such as *dtSearch*[39] and look to see if you dreamt of the same people, places or things before. You can employ word-search for this. Use your journal to gain further insight by occasionally reading back over past dreams and comments.[40] This can be enormously helpful and strengthening, especially at times when you are making important decisions or are confused.

Opening the Dream Door
One of the most immediate ways of understanding your dreams is to

ask yourself, or be asked, the right questions. Here are some points to raise about the dream:

1. *What is the background to the dream?* The feelings triggered by everyday events may have contributed to the dream. Ask yourself if there are parts of the dream that have similar feelings to your everyday life. You may be meeting particular events or inner feelings. This can often be a stimulant to a dream.

2. *What is the main action in the dream?* How would you describe what you are doing in the dream? Are you walking, looking, worrying, building something or trying to escape? Define what it is and give it a name, such as those listed, or something like 'Waiting' — 'Searching' — 'Following'. Then ask yourself if this applies in any way to your waking life. Are you 'waiting' or 'following'? If so, is that what you want? Do not forget that the dream represents events in a figurative way, so building a house can be summarised as 'Building'. The question would therefore be 'What are you building in your life at the moment?'

3. *What is your role in the dream?* Roles are important in dreams as they often tell us what we feel we are doing at the moment. Are you a friend, lover, soldier, dictator, watcher or drop-out in the dream? Take time to consider how the role you define applies to you. Do not forget that all the characters in the dream are parts of yourself, so don't discard the roles of other people. They represent subsidiary activities or attitudes to your main one.

4. *Are you active or passive in the dream?* Are you letting others take the lead, or are you dominated or indecisive in the dream? Such attitudes may reflect your waking habits of responding to others. Examine them. You can change what you dream by becoming aware of passivity. This will affect your everyday life. See Question 8.

5. *What do you feel in the dream?* Your feelings are very important in dreams. They are one of the main structures around which everything else is woven. Take time to define them, or even what feelings are suggested by the action of the dream. Then consider whether you are acknowledging them in your waking life, and what part they play.

6. *Am I Meeting the Things I Am Afraid of in My Dream?* When something frightening moves towards you in a dream, it means the

fear or pain it depicts is becoming more conscious or felt. To run away or try to escape is only a means of suppressing the anxiety again. Maybe that is what you want to do. But if not, stop running away. Meet the creature or thing that threatens. This allows enormous healing and growth to occur. Without facing the aspects you fear in your dreams, you gradually build up more and more of yourself that is repressed. See Question 8. Of course, you can turn to meet your fear gradually.

7. *What Have I Mistakenly Introverted?* We often perform actions in our dreams that have no place there. For example, we may dream of falling into the sea and be terrified we will drown. That is ridiculous because we can easily breathe under water in a dream, or fly, or die and be reborn. The sea we fear drowning in, the sky we fear falling from, the monsters we flee, are our own emotions. We drown in sorrow, we fall in our own estimation and we may run from responsibility or decisions. Learning to breathe under water, to fly, to confront monsters in our dreams is a way of discovering how to handle our feelings just like a sailor learns to handle the sea. It is a life skill.

8. *How Can I Alter the Dream to Find Greater Satisfaction?* Having asked the preceding questions, you may have become aware that parts of your dream are unsatisfying. You might be confused, in a changing situation that has not been resolved, or avoiding something. You could be running away or being passive. Whatever it is, ask what you would do if you could satisfy yourself. Then imagine yourself in the dream and change what happened. Literally try out different ways of carrying the dream forward to a satisfying conclusion. Do not just cut out the 'bad' bits. There are no bad bits in dreams. Aim to find a feeling in which you can sense a real change, a real shifting of tension or dissatisfaction. Experiment till you discover it.

9. *What does the dream mean?* Nobody but you creates your dream characters and environment while you sleep. Therefore, by stepping into each of the dream people, animals and places, you can discover out of what emotions, memories or ideas you created them. In a playful, relaxed way, express whatever you think, feel, remember or fantasise when you hold each part of the dream in mind. Say or write it all, even the seemingly trivial or 'dangerous'

bits. For instance, as a house you might describe yourself as 'a bit old, but with open doors for family and friends to come in and out. I feel solid and dependable, but I sense there is something hidden in my cellar.' Such statements portray yourself graphically. Consider whatever information you gather as descriptive of your waking life. More description will be added to this technique later. Whenever possible talk in the first person, even as a tree — 'I am a tree. I am quite a young tree. I am still waiting for my leaf buds to open,' etc.

10. *Summarise.* Gather the essence of what you have said about each part of your dream and express it in everyday language. Imagine you are explaining to someone who knows nothing about yourself or the dream. Bring the dream out of its symbols into everyday comments concerning yourself. A man dreamt about a grey, dull office. When he looked at what he said about the office, he realised he was talking about the grey, unimaginative world in which he grew up after the Second World War, and how it shaped him.[41]

The Dream Interview
Gayle Delaney developed an approach called the 'Dream interview'.[42] It can be practised alone, with another person, or with a group. It is a technique that is useful for almost anyone. Fundamentally you, or your interviewer, ask basic questions about the dream as, for instance, the questions in the previous section. The difference is that you write them down or speak out aloud. Some of Delaney's basic questions are:
1. What do you feel about the dream?
2. Describe and relate the settings to waking life.
3. Who is each dream person? What is he or she like?
4. What is each dream object? What is it like?
5. How does each feeling, person or object relate to waking life?
6. Describe the dream events. What do they remind you of in your present life?

The 'Dream interview' technique overlaps with what will be described in the next section so read on for further information about using the technique.

Be Your Own Dream Detective

The following approach emerged from my work over thirty years, and that of Dr Dina Glouberman, lecturer in psychology.[43] It is designed to be used with one or more people acting as your helper(s). It is a powerfully effective approach as good as — or better — than visiting a £30-an-hour therapist! After being the subject adopting this method, a professional Jungian once told me: 'When I get home I am going to start a group using this approach. I am fed up with my dreams being ripped to shreds by colleagues.'

As Delaney repeats again and again, you are the expert on your dreams. With help from friends who can learn this approach, you will discover the thrill and uplift of entering dreams. It is important to use each step as it is explained. If you stay with the guide-lines you will get excellent results. It does need your helper and yourself to be inquisitive, and to take time to be a dream detective.[44]

Step One — Find a partner or group you can relax with who can give sympathetic and non-intrusive support. Get agreement from your partner(s) that any confidences disclosed during the dream exploration will not be told to others.

Step Two — Tell your dream to your partner or group. It helps if you relate it in the first person present as if you are experiencing the dream as you tell it. Describing the dream can include any relevant information, such as immediate associations, events directly or feelings linked with the dream. Here is an example:

> I am in Watkins's bookshop in London. I feel Mr Watkins is a very rational man, and I am asking his advice concerning a woman about whom I feel confused. I am confused because she is constantly ill at ease with me or muddled, or I am at odds with her. Watkins tells me that she is like that with everyone and I must not take it personally. In other words, I am okay and not producing tension and disagreement in people generally. I feel better on hearing this as I have been living with a sense that something is wrong with me in relationships.

If Ben, the dreamer, had talked in the past tense and said, 'I *was* in Watkins's bookshop — I *felt* confused — I *was* at odds', the effect would not have been nearly as immediate. The difference in telling it in the first person present is that Ben admits such things as 'I *am* at odds, I *am* confused'. Telling the dream often enables you immediately to link the feeling with a waking situation. Because the dreamer needs to explain any associations or waking links with the dream, Ben told his helpers that he was in a relationship with a woman about whom he felt uncertain. He was losing confidence in his ability to be okay in the relationship.

Step Three — The helpers now ask you questions to clarify for themselves the imagery and drama of the dream. At this point, the questions should not be to explore the dream, but simply to gain a clear image of it and what happens.

The helper needs a full picture and a feeling about the dream to ask the most helpful questions in the steps that follow. Taking the example dream, the helper might ask Ben, 'What age is Mr Watkins?' Ben would say he is an older man than himself. This, with the information that Mr Watkins is rational, helps to set the scene. You might also try to get a clearer view of the bookshop, or whether other people were present. Do not make this step too long or conversational. It is used to get an all-round view on which to build good questions.

Step Four — You now choose one of the people, places or things in the dream to explore. It is important to realise that it does not matter if the dream person or place is someone/something known or not. The character needs to be treated as an aspect of your dream, and not as if he or she were the living person exterior to the dream. Usually, you choose the most interesting or major part of the dream. In the example, Ben could choose to investigate feelings and associations about Mr Watkins, the bookshop or himself. He could also explore the 'elderly woman' mentioned. It does not matter that she doesn't appear in the dream. She is present as feelings and influence.

Step Five — You now stand in the role of the dream character or thing you have decided to probe. If you chose to be a car that appeared in the dream, you would close your eyes, enter into the feeling sense and imagery of the dream, and describe yourself as the car. Again, this needs to be done in first person present. Here is an example using Ben's dream:

> As Mr Watkins, Ben said: 'I have a lot of experience of people and their ideas, and am acquainted with the spiritual dimension of life, too. I feel slightly irritated with Ben as he lets himself get so influenced by his emotions'.

> Exploring himself in the dream Ben said: 'I feel confused and really want help with what is happening. In fact, I am feeling like this in my everyday life, but I haven't sought an authority figure like Watkins. I feel he is a bit impatient with me, but what he is telling me helps.'

Although Ben knew Watkins in his waking life, he needs to stay mostly with what happens in the dream and not stray off into a long description of the external Watkins. At this step, Ben could already see what his dream was about. To some extent, he had already acknowledged his difficulty in the relationship prior to the dream, but it focused his attention on the possibility that the situation might not be all his fault. Also, he had not admitted how much the relationship problem was bothering him.

Step Six — The helpers now ask questions while you stay in the role of the dream character or thing. The questions must be directly related to the role you, the dreamer, are in. They should always remain simple and connected with the dream imagery and drama. For instance, if the dream character was a dog, you could usefully ask such questions as, 'Are you an old or young dog? Are you male or female? What do you like doing as a dog? What do you feel about the human you are with?'

It is not helpful to take the dreamer out of role by asking such points as, 'Do you know a dog like this? Do you think this dog represents your sexual feelings?' Instead, they could be phrased like this: 'What sort of dog character are you? Are you a sexy sort of dog?' The questions are best if they relate to what happens in the dream to help the dreamer uncover more information about it and his or her feelings.

When Ben is in the role of Watkins he could be asked: 'What sort of person are you (as Watkins)? Is there something else you want to say to Ben? How do you know about spiritual subjects? Why do you think Ben has got himself in this fix? What are you doing in this shop?'

If you are working in a group, take care to let the dreamer respond in his or her own time. If a question is producing results, do not ask another question that leads them right off in another direction. Help deepen their experience. Mine the vein of gold. Dreamers often touch strong feelings, so give the subject time to feel them by allowing him or her to laugh, cry, be silent, etc.

Work through each of the dream symbols in the time you allow yourself. Then permit space to summarise by asking the dreamer what he or she gathered from exploring each part of their dream. Particularly help them to compare what they discovered from the dream with their waking life and its concerns.

As the dreamer, do not hold back from saying whatever comes to mind or expressing any feelings that arise. People exploring their dream like this have often said, 'But what I am saying may not be right.' It does not matter. Put it out as if you are laying the pieces of information on a table in front of you. When you summarise, you can link the information gathered to what is important and real in your life.

Whatever information you arrive at — for instance, Ben saw how much his feelings of being no good in his relationship were bothering him, and how necessary it was to deal with the issue — take time to consider what you want to do about it. Ask yourself what changes you can usefully make. Ben decided not to keep 'beating himself up' with the notion that he was a failure.

The Drama of Your Dreams

Dreams are usually snippets of drama with a beginning, middle and end. This is one of the reasons many researchers reject the idea of their being random. Like a TV play or a film, your dreams are masters of lighting, setting and intimation. I remember watching the film *The Thing* with my youngest son, and seeing how the drama was intensified and suggested by darkness. As the terror was resolved, so the lighting got brighter. In just the same way, dreams use lighting and setting to describe our internal world of mind and emotions. This following sequence from a dream illustrates this:

> As I am walking, I meet this man by coincidence. I immediately begin to worry he is going to rob me, especially in one dark area through which we have to pass. When we get to the dark area, it suddenly turns light and there is a swimming pool next to an hotel. There are a lot of people around.

In this extract, the changing emotions from the dark to the light are clear to see. The difficulty for you might be to connect what is felt in the dream with waking life. In many cases, this may simply be because you have not admitted even to yourself what the dream portrays. Also, to admit it intellectually is often not enough. You may need to feel it, to experience it, for yourself. Remember that you are not just a mind, not just a body, not just emotions, not just pleasant or unpleasant sense experiences, not just a part of a huge complex and mysterious universe — you are all of these aspects at once! However, usually you tend to live in just one or two parts of yourself.

Some of the most powerful ways of experiencing yourself more fully and discovering the wholeness of your dream are to use drama and movement.

Acting In
Extracting more from your dream by letting your body and feelings express it can provide a remarkable release of insight. There are several ways of doing this.

Walk On Part — This is the simplest method. It requires you to play with your imagination a little and go along with a fantasy, the sort of talent we all develop as children. If you have a sympathetic audience it helps, but only if you feel comfortable in front of others. It is fine alone as well. Stand with your eyes closed in the middle of enough space to move around. About two or three square metres are usually plenty.

Imagine you are standing on the edge of your dream, like a film set, and you are going to walk into it. Before you actually step into your dream, be aware of what you are feeling in your body and emotions. Your body and feelings are a screen upon which subtle changes and shifts will occur. It is this screen of body and emotions that will act as your monitor, showing what responses your dream produces.

Now step into your dream. Literally step forward. Walk about in the 'film set' of your dream, watching what you feel, what memories come and what you fantasise. Talk with the characters. Even imagine stepping into their bodies and register what feelings and intuitions they produce on your screen of body and feelings. Speak what you feel and find to your helpers or tape recorder. You can enter into anything in this way, whether it is an animal, a tree, the sea or a house. You can ask questions as you explore your dream in this way. Your intuition will play its responses on the monitor of your body and emotions. The possibilities are that you enter the dream and explore its different places and people, or you re-live the dream by acting it out.

This Is How It Was — In many dreams you, the dreamer, or one of the characters, expresses something dramatic or ordinary that can be used as a doorway to insight. As an example, Kelly had the following dream:

> I am in an exotic foreign shop, but the owner does not understand me. Then he speaks English. I laugh, and start jumping around saying, 'You can understand me'.

Kelly could take up the posture she had in the dream and act it by saying out aloud, 'You don't understand me!' This would need to be repeated a few times with as much of the feeling of frustration or attitudes connected with being misunderstood as appeared in, or were suggested, by the dream. What this can do is to involve more of yourself in expression than you do usually. This brings to the surface feelings that may otherwise be difficult to be aware of. Once felt, they can be recognised for what they are. Often what happens is that the acting-out carries on from the dream, and may even involve some life situation in which you have been. In other words, you act or feel something more than was in the dream. Kelly could also try 'jumping around' shouting 'You can understand me!'

The aim is to dramatise what the dream is expressing to see if we can find what part of our history or emotions it is depicting. This often 'hooks' memories or feelings that would otherwise not be discovered.

Another approach is to take up the posture or movement in the dream. I was a helper once with Dave, who dreamt of a policeman sitting astride a powerful motor-bike. Dave failed to understand this part of the dream using other methods, so we built a pile of cushions for him to sit astride. He sat there for a while. When we asked how he felt, he said, 'Powerful!' Dave had been feeling a lack of power to do things or to accomplish anything. As he acted out the posture and feeling of being on the bike, he could 'feel' the power in his body and the confidence in himself to do what he wanted. It was not simply the dream confidence, but Dave's own strength he could now experience.

As suggested with Dave, this acting out can be a group action. None of us actually got in on the act with him, but sometimes it helps to get other people involved in the drama, as when you want someone to resist or to hold.

A memorable example was with Olive. A dream scene in which she was sitting opposite a woman in a café puzzled her. Latent in the scene was something to do with love, but Olive could not 'get it'. I suggested she sit opposite Hy, a woman partner, and asked Olive repeatedly to say to Hy, 'Please love me.' The effect was enormous. All the feelings Olive had buried about wanting love from her mother surfaced and were felt. It was a very healing experience.

And Then What? — A technique that is occasionally very helpful is to carry the dream forward. This has already been mentioned in Question 8. As it is so useful, further information will be given.

It is particularly relevant when the end of the dream is not satisfying or doesn't resolve the feelings or issue expressed. The method is simple. Imagine yourself in the dream and continue it as a fantasy or day-dream. You can alter the dream in any way you want. Continue the plot forward to some sort of conclusion or resolution. But it is important to watch your feelings to see whether what you do is satisfying and feels right. It might be a defensive change you make instead of a creative one.

Be aware if there is any anger or hostility in the dream that are not fully expressed. If so, let yourself imagine a full expression of the anger. Look for the feeling of satisfaction. This occurs only as you learn to acknowledge and integrate resistances and anxieties regarding what you express. It will not arise if you fail to face your fears or deal with the feelings that are trying to resolve in the dream.

This is a very important method. Moving the dream forward like this removes habits which trap you in lack of satisfaction, poor creativity or inability to resolve problems. Using it, you can turn to face the situations from which you have been running. You can get hold of the dream lover who has always eluded you before. You can catch that train, open that door, get to the top of the stairs and do all the things that anxiety, habit or low self-esteem were holding you back from. This can change your life. But to achieve it, you must face, feel and admit what has been retarding you.

Moving Into Your Dream

Being able to move and feel alive are tightly bound together. All the life processes in us express as movement of one sort or another. To breathe, to laugh, to make love and to feel anger or joy is to move.

When any important life-movements, such as those taking place in the intestines, heart or genitals, are inhibited we are less alive, less healthy. Every emotion we feel has its corresponding movement in action, a body posture or subtle changes in our muscles. When powerful emotions such as love or anger are not expressed, they become 'held-back movement'. We usually call this tension.

As such tension deepens, it becomes psychosomatic illness — pain without apparent physical malfunction. In its worse form, it manifests as real illness. Amongst the most common 'movements' we hold back are those connected with love, sex, anger, fear, crying, emotional pain and sometimes even laughter and joy. In dreams, we often attempt to express movements that are suppressed during our waking life. Unfortunately, our habits of tension are so deep that we may not manage to release them even while asleep.

Freud was one of the first indirectly to point this out when he brought attention to how often people who are sexually repressed symbolise the sex act in dreams. He found that even in sleep the person could not allow a sexual experience. Put another way, there are certain situations we cannot face. This is how dreams depict it. We dream of shutting a door on something, run away, wake up in fear or put the emotion or desire outside us in the form of another person or event.

In most important life-movements, such as breathing, our body moves spontaneously. We do not need to make it happen. This is what takes place in dreams, too. But as the movement may be only partly expressed in life or in dreams, it is incredibly healing to let your dream process express more freely while awake. Jung spoke of this when he said that our conscious personality 'appears intent on blotting out spontaneous fantasy that might reveal something other than its own cherished defences and beliefs'. He said that the ways people get beyond this block are different. 'In most cases the results of these efforts are not very encouraging at first . . . oftentimes the hands alone can fantasy; they model or draw figures that are quite foreign to the conscious'.[45]

If you are deeply committed to discovering what dreams can reveal, letting such spontaneous movement happen[46] increases your depth of communication with your dreaming self. An easy way of starting to learn this is to experiment with the difference between, for example, lifting your arms above your head firstly as a willed movement, then as one arising from being aware what your body wants to do. Take your time with this. Do it over and over until you find how different a willed movement is to a spontaneous one. Learning to allow a good yawn also helps. Try a few 'acted' yawns to see if you can let a natural one emerge.

Once you know how to let this happen, you are ready to hold a dream character or object in mind and let your body express spontaneously what it wants to in connection with the dream. If there is a movement in the dream, such as pushing something away or struggling, this approach is particularly relevant.

Marilyn had a dream in which a dinosaur stood in her path, devouring all who approached it. She thought the dream must hide some sort of aggression so we explored it by asking Marilyn to find a body posture and movements which for her expressed the feeling of the dinosaur. When she did this, Marilyn didn't express anger or aggression with her body. As the dinosaur, she felt like a predator that always had to take to get her own needs.

This feeling immediately reminded her of family life as a child. Marilyn remembered one time when she was sent shopping aged three or four. As well as buying what she had been asked, she purchased some sweets for herself. When Marilyn arrived home, she was treated as if she had done something terrible: that was where she began to feel like a predator. It seemed to her as if her needs were always gained at the expense of someone else. As that was a prime issue in her life, Marilyn managed to learn from the experience and went on to fulfil her needs without feeling guilty.

Dream Incubation
To incubate a dream means to seek earnestly for one that responds to a special need or question. This way of approaching the best in yourself for help has been practised widely in many cultures. Some evidence suggests it was first used as a means of curing sterility, and was widespread enough to be employed by Australian aborigines as well as Chinese and North Africans.

It evolved into a much wider application. In more recent history its various uses range from young women seeking to dream about their future husband to Amerindian youths fasting in lonely vigil to receive a dream about their inmost character and destiny. Many such approaches, such as those used in Ancient Greece in the healing temples of Aesculapius,[47] were felt to be sacred. Individuals were helped to take on a feeling of approaching the divine and humbly seeking aid from the highest wisdom. The effectiveness of this is to be found in many historical records.

In today's world we have no dream incubation temples. Moreover, our culture does not often encourage us to take a cleansing fast and vigil to incubate a dream. We may not have learned the humility and joy felt in approaching the sacred. But as individuals we can still recognise that the forces behind nature and our own existence are special and potent. The great cycles of birth and death, or mating and reproduction, are to be seen everywhere, springing from eternal powers. To approach the fount of these with reverence is not irrational. To seek deeper understanding of your own life situation, your health or your relationship with the whole can still bring wonderful blessings and change.

To apply this yourself, the first step is to recognise that the unconscious processes of your mind and body, of your transcendent self, are not like a machine into which you can drop a coin, press a button and out pops a can of Coke. The unconscious can be helpfully likened to a person. It is intelligent, responsive and moved by meaningful communication and sympathy. To gain the help of this potent power in yourself, you need its co-operation.

The second step is to remember your dreams and see if they are already dealing with the subject upon which you want information. It may be that your unconscious has other matters that need attention first, so think around the question you want answered. Recognise the feelings surrounding it. A frivolous point that does not connect with the important issues of your life will not easily get the attention of your unconscious. The more vital the question is — either for your own welfare or work — the more likely it is that your unconscious will explore the issue and present a dream response.

When you have a reasonable respect for what you are approaching, define your question. Write it carefully as a letter to your unconscious and place it under your pillow. Expect a reply as you would from a good friend. Your unconscious is your best and loving friend. It knows you intimately as does no one else. When you wake, pause and let any dream flow into awareness. Record it immediately in some way. Then explore it as suggested in the sections in The Dream Interview and Be Your Own Dream Detective. Try again if you do not get a response the first time.

Lucid Dreaming

The word 'lucid' in connection with dreaming means becoming aware that you are dreaming while still in the dream. There are several levels and possibilities, ranging from the amusing to the profound.

An aspect many people experience is where they are dreaming of something that produces anxiety. They then wake enough to realise they are dreaming and change the dream to something pleasant. Although a number of writers about dreams recommend this type of lucidity, considering the amount of evidence we have that burying emotions such as grief or anxiety produces illness, repressing the feelings by changing them does not seem the best solution.

Another type of lucid dreaming is where the dreamer becomes awake in the dream, but is not avoiding anything. Again, popular comment on this level of lucidity suggests playing with the dream by changing it or creating dream lovers with whom to have wonderful sex. To be able to transform your own feelings and attitudes by altering the images representing them is certainly a good exercise. Its lessons need to be carried over into waking life so that when a negative attitude appears, the process of change used in the dream is applied.

The most profound level of lucidity is to recognise you are dreaming, then discover what the dream drama and imagery hold within them about yourself. Out of what part of your history, out of what mental and emotional process and quality, out of what fear or pain, out of what unconscious splendours of your being, has this dream taken form? The aim is to melt the symbols to see from what they arise.

If it is remembered that abilities such as dream telepathy and out-of-the-body experiences occur while in a lucid state — i.e. being awake while asleep — the possibilities of lucidity may be glimpsed. To give some idea of what can be found through lucid dreaming, I summarise a feature written by Oliver W. Markley that first appeared in *Whole Earth Review*, Fall 1991. Oliver recalls what he saw while in a lucid state. He described the experience as a looking back at the projector producing the 'movie' of the dream, enabling him to witness from where the movie was arising. I have paraphrased some of Oliver's comments:

> I saw there are five categories of experience in the dream state. 'The function of the first type of dream process I saw was pure entertainment.' This is like the pleasure and information we gain from watching TV. The second category of dreaming was a review of unfinished business and current concerns in an attempt to find solutions. The third process is similar to the second, but at a deeper level. It is concerned with getting an overview of your life to balance it with the wider life of the world, and the way your individual life meshes with the whole. It deals with your growth, destiny and their outworking in everyday life.
>
> The fourth mode is a sort of gymnasium for the mind and spirit. It exercises those aspects of yourself not used in daily life. The final and fifth type of dream is akin to being visited by aliens in that it is a meeting place for all that lies beyond the framework of our conscious concepts of what is real, where we meet minds beyond our ken.

Although these aspects of dreaming were described in the first chapter in other ways, linking them with lucid dreaming reminds us that to access them consciously enables you to use them more fully. The simple method of becoming more lucid in your dreams is basically to keep penetrating your dreams with awareness by probing them while awake. Consistently exploring your dreams to extract insight *is* a form of lucidity. Like Oliver, you discover what produced the movie of your dream. If you carry this attitude into dreaming by deepening your skill at using the tools of insight, you begin to wake up in your sleep. Particularly relevant are the techniques described under *Walk on Part and Moving in to Your Dream*. These enable you to penetrate the symbols of your dreams and become aware of the underlying emotions and intuitions. This growing awareness will stimulate greater lucidity in dreams.

Three techniques that can increase lucidity are as follows. This first is described by Castle.[48] You wear a wrist-watch that will give an audible signal. Set it to sound every ninety minutes. When it does so, stare at it intently for a few moments, asking yourself whether you are awake or asleep. The ninety-minute cycle is the same as dreaming. By wearing the watch at night, or placing it near your bed, you will hear the signal. Through the habit of looking at it during the day, you will be cued to look at it while you dream. The question of whether you are awake or not will help you to become lucid.

The second technique was designed by LaBerge,[49] an expert on lucidity. Whenever you wake from a dream, immediately imagine yourself back within it and create the image and feelings of yourself becoming lucid in the dream. As you do this, say to yourself, 'Next time I dream I will recognise I am dreaming.'

Thirdly, use any type of meditation or relaxation technique that enables you to quieten your mind and body. When you have reached the quiet state, repeat to yourself several times the affirmation: 'I will become aware in my dreams. I will carry awareness into my dreams and use this awareness to heal myself and become whole.'

The overall effect of this is to increase enormously the efficiency and speed with which your personal growth and effectiveness in the world occur. The main advantage of becoming lucid in your sleep rather than while exploring a dream awake is that it is easier to travel the farther reaches of insight, such as extended perception, into dream imagery.

These techniques also lend themselves to the exploration of out-of-body experiences (OBE). To attempt an OBE, recognise that you are trying to enter a new world of experience. The first time I had a conscious OBE, I was terrified I was dying. If you recognise that you might meet such a sensation before you start, when you face it the feeling will quickly disperse and you can continue with the OBE. My fear melted as soon as I realised it was an OBE rather than a terminal experience.

When you achieve lucidity, you can use the watch method as a focus for the OBE. As the watch gives a signal and you gaze at it, instead of asking the question of whether you are awake or not, concentrate on the words: 'Now I am becoming lucid in my dream. I am free to project my awareness to anywhere or anyone I wish.' When an OBE happens, a lot of the action is spontaneous, like any process streaming from the unconscious. But it can be spontaneous along pre-planned lines. Take time before you go to sleep to build a mental picture and feelings about where you want to go, or whom you wish to visit. If there are any really good reasons, like an urgent message or healing to someone, you wish to convey in the OBE, the unconscious is more likely to put its shoulder behind your effort.

Summary
Like a selection of tools in a tool-box, the different techniques are useful in approaching dreams from various standpoints. Talking over a dream and discovering the life situations and feelings you associate with it can reveal satisfying insights. But some dreams are not about a present life circumstance, or if they are, the dream may be showing that a long past hurt in childhood needs to be resolved before the situation can change. With such a dream, it might not be enough to come to an intellectual understanding.

You may need to remember by re-experiencing the powerful childhood emotions that burned particular reactions into you. For instance, a child who was abandoned in an orphanage had the emotion of waiting and trying to be good etched into him, along with self-destructive anger regarding women. The need for love and his anger were in conflict. Those emotions were so deeply buried he had to feel them again to realise what they were doing in his life, and to redirect his reactions. Group-work in such cases is enormously helpful, especially when coupled with the acting-in approach.

The spontaneous movement approach is most helpful when part of a dream remains mysterious and without insight, despite all your efforts. This is because it can reveal the unconscious through mime, non-verbal expression and by going beyond consciously held opinions and viewpoint.

5
Dream Meanings

Gayle Delaney echoes the attitude of many therapists when she says, 'We all dream our own private images, and no dream dictionary can tell you what the dream means.' Certainly, some dream dictionaries, as already mentioned, are written from a superstitious background. However, Freud wrote a dream dictionary, and many high-standing dream analysts base their interpretation of a dream on well-established definitions of common dream images. For instance, in Jungian analysis a female in a man's dream can represent the anima, the female component in every man. A square shape might symbolise wholeness or stability.

A good analyst will not apply such background information rigidly to the dreamer. However, knowledge of such meaning will be used as an enormously helpful guide in asking the right questions. There is no reason you cannot do the same with your own dreams. Knowing what the different characters, creatures, places and objects might depict can guide you to look in the right area of your life to see what the dream may refer to.

This chapter describes the various broad categories into which your dream images and dramas fall. The definitions have been arrived at by summarising the results of thousands of dream interviews. For example, what different people report about their own dream of the sea is often very similar. You may find that the way you use the sea in your dream might be similar to the given definition. Even if not precisely the same, the definition will start you thinking and can lead to your own insight. By looking at the possible meaning of each of your dream images, you can get an overall idea of to what your dream might refer. Then you need to examine the area of your life to which this points to see if you can make the connection with your waking life.

The Dream Guide

Before attempting to understand your dream by looking at how dream images are commonly used, there is an important starting point. To get the best from what follows, do not take any of the suggested definitions and rigidly apply them to yourself. Dreams are usually very specific. If the definition suggests you are worried about your work or partner, ask yourself if this is so. If it is, look again at the dream to see what comment it is making about this worry. Dreams seldom re-state the obvious. They usually give an insightful view of the situation as well. By 'comment' is meant the context and feeling tone of the dream.

The aim of this chapter is not to make you dependent on these ready-made definitions of dream images, so prior to each section a way of looking at the subject is given that will assist you to define for yourself what the dream image may be describing in your life circumstances. Then a definition is supplied to help you see how the image might be used in some dreams.

In considering your dream in this way, the first step is to grasp the overall theme and feeling of the dream before any particular images are looked at. To do this, use the questions given in Chapter Four under *Opening The Dream Door*. Particularly note what the feeling tone of the dream is, what your role and action in the dream are, and what the dramatic theme of the dream is. When you have done this, ask yourself how these apply to your everyday life. The following example gives an idea of this.

> I remember leaving some place and embarking on a journey at night. I am frightened, but want to make this trip. I approach a stream with a very narrow bridge. It is dark. I am afraid I may fall off the bridge. But to continue, I must cross the bridge — R.

In this dream, R is undertaking some sort of change in her life: the journey. There is great uncertainty about what it is. This is shown by the darkness, whilst R's anxiety suggests a change arising from factors other than her choice. In this process, R is facing anxiety and possibly constraints — the narrow bridge. The dream suggests that to make the change successfully, she must carry on despite the anxiety. The feeling tone of the dream is one of difficulty and encouragement. The role is that of a traveller or adventurer. The dramatic theme is of facing difficulty in change. With this information R can now ask herself: 'What change am I facing in my waking life? Am I aware of feeling anxious about this? What are the constraints, difficulties or "bridge" to cross? How can I carry on despite my fears?'

As can be seen, defining the dream in this way, and then asking how it applies to waking life, almost immediately brings clear insights. This is especially so if, when you summarise the dream, you put your description in everyday language. This is very important when you come to translating phrases such as 'narrow bridge' into something other than a cliché. For instance, if, like R, you dreamt of a narrow bridge, what would it mean? If you take away the cliché, it might symbolise that your progress is getting harder or more restricting. This same translation of imagery into everyday language is important in connection with dream drama, too. You can see how this is achieved in R's dream. The drama of a night journey is put into the words of anxiety and change.

People
People appear in your dreams more often than anything else, apart from yourself. To get your own idea of what a person or a group of people mean in your dream, take time to think how you use the words 'person' or 'people' in everyday language. Some examples are, 'I feel like a new person' and 'What sort of person is he/she?' Apart from the direct use of the word *person*, we indirectly refer to our personality when making remarks like, 'I don't know what came over me to do something like that.' In our dreams, we literally use the image of another person to describe these 'other' aspects of our personality. We especially employ friends and family to do this as their personality traits and weaknesses are well known to us. So consider what sort of person is in your dream, and his or her character traits. Then ask yourself what aspect of yourself is depicted. Here are further descriptions to help you:

You — How you appear in the dream may depict your self-image or the way you feel about yourself at the time of the dream or in connection with the dream theme.

A Person — An aspect of your own personality or feelings. By defining what character the person in the dream has, you define what aspect of yourself. For example, a banker would suggest your ability to deal with money or concerns about it. A person you know who is talented might indicate your own abilities, etc. *Somebody you know in a particular role in the dream*: This may mean you are seeing them — or trying to put them — into that role, with your mother as a witch or partner as lazy.

Authority Figure — By what authority do you live? What rules or beliefs give you strength or restrict you? The authority figure might represent the moral or social code in which you were trained as a child or even your parents' attitudes that you battle with in trying to be an individual.

Baby or Child — Feelings or memories from your infancy or childhood. If it is your own baby or child, it may be your feelings and worries about them, but more often it is your vulnerable feelings or dependence.

Dead People or People from Your Past — The influence of individuals still active in you. Haunting memories. Feelings about death.

Enemy — What powerful attitudes or guilt do you fight with? Is the enemy an older person reminding you of a parent? Are you in conflict with something within yourself?

Ghost — Memories from the past haunting you.

Group of People — Not feeling alone. Different aspects of yourself. Sociability. Involvement with others.

Man — *In a woman's dream*: Feelings about men, or a particular man. Your own male qualities, such as abilities in the world. See *A Person*. *In a man's dream*: An aspect of your own personality, depending on the character of the person. See *A Person*.

Old Person — Depending on the gender, it can depict feelings about your mother or father. Wisdom of experience. Feelings about ageing.

Young Person — Growth. Feelings, attitudes and difficulties you had at that age.

Events with People

Wedding — This can literally signify marriage, such as when a single woman or man thinks, worries or speculates about getting wed. In this case, the dream would be an outline of their fears and perhaps a way to deal with anxieties, or what the cause is of the worry. It can also be about finding unity within yourself, as between thinking and feeling, conscious and unconscious.

Birth — The birth of a child often represents something new and promising emerging in your life. This might be a relationship, an opportunity, an idea or some new aspect of your personality. In a woman's dream, it may indicate her feelings about giving birth or wanting a baby. If pregnant at the time of the dream, it often signifies worries or feelings about the baby.

Funeral — People often dream of witnessing their own funeral. This is because we all wonder about death, and so sometimes practise it in our dreams. Seeing someone else buried might be a hidden wish 'to get rid of them'. Very occasionally, it is a premonition about the person's health. A funeral may also represent the end of something in your life, like a relationship or mourning for someone dead.

Party — Your social ability, i.e. how you deal with groups. Looking for sexual partner. Social pleasure.

Walking with Family — This depicts the relationship with your family. The events in the dream will show what difficulties or strengths you have.

> ### MO'S BABY
>
> 'I gave birth to a baby girl I named Charlotte. I had mixed emotions about this, uncertainty, excitement. I wanted to share the news with my friends. I phoned a friend, but she listened quietly and remained silent. I felt uneasy, then the friend said "We lost Luke" — her son — "the week before". I then woke with muddled feelings.'
>
> The death that happened the 'week before' was that Mo had split with a lover. The new baby is the possibility of life outside the relationship.

The Body

In dreams, your body shows what sort of self-image you possess. This means that even the most insignificant dream in which you have any awareness of what you look like or your body shape is a reflection of largely unconscious concepts and feelings about yourself. You may mistake this self-image for reality, and believe this is how others see you. In fact, there is no stable 'real' self, either in how you feel about yourself or how others see you.

If you watch your feelings during the day, your sense of self shifts minute by minute. But how you see yourself is of prime importance.

This is because your self-image is often so deeply unconscious you may believe it is a reality and act as if it is true. Therefore, take time to look at what your dreams show about your self-image and re-evaluate it.

Parts of your body depict the various aspects of your mind and emotions. Ask yourself what each part is used for. This clarifies its meaning in your dreams.

Hair: Thoughts. The image you present of yourself.

Head: Your mind and reasoning. Your identity and public image. Self-control — 'Lost my head'.

Eyes: Ability to know. Your inner moods. Connection with other people, as in 'eye-to-eye'.

> **MOTHER'S NOSE**
>
> 'I dreamt my mother was strangling me with her nose. Her nose was pressed right into my neck, stopping me breathing' — Celine.
>
> Celine's dream shows the nose being used to represent being nosy. Celine was fifteen at the time of the dream. She agreed that her mother was being over curious about what she was doing.

Nose: Sensing events or situations, therefore intuition and curiosity. Feelings that lead you on, as with an exciting smell.

Teeth: Your 'bite' or power in the world. Losing your teeth often depicts anxiety concerning appearance, about how others see you.

Mouth: What you express in words. Your hungers. Sexual excitement and sensuality. Also your ability to take things into you, such as hurtful remarks. Pulling something out of the mouth shows you removing what has perhaps 'got into you' from other people's remarks or what you have read.

Neck: Vulnerability. Link between feelings and thoughts, sexuality and reasoning. *Idioms*: Breaking your neck; Up to your neck; Risk your neck; Stick your neck out; Dead from the neck up/down.

Shoulders/Back: Strength. Ability to 'carry' the load of life experience.

Arms: Your ability to give and receive. Capacity to support or defend, to hold on or push away. Your 'doing' power in the world.

Hands: Your hold on life, people, the world. Power to extend your skills, love, anger and healing. Contact with people and the world. What you have. Idioms: Second-hand; In the hands of; Bite the hand that feeds; Hands are tied; Soil your hands; Hand-to-hand; Hand-to-mouth; Hands off; Hard hand; Helping hand; Open-handed; Lend a hand; Upper hand; Burnt fingers; At your fingertips; Snap your fingers; Green fingers; Have a finger in; Itchy fingers; Sticky fingers; Fingers crossed; Lay a finger on; Point the finger at; Get your finger out; Fingers to the bone.

Chest: Emotions. Feelings you store in your 'chest' from years past. Therefore, anything sticking in the chest or connected with it usually depicts emotions or stuck emotions expressing themselves as psychosomatic discomfort. Condition of chest also indicates social confidence or pride. See: Breathing.

Breathing: Difficulties in breathing link with anxiety or fear of death. In some cases, this connects with a difficult birth. Also feelings about restriction or frustration. When positive in the dream, breathing shows you taking in life, feeling at ease with your environment.

Breasts: Giving of yourself or being given to. Sexual pleasure or enticement. The breast, for a woman, provides a sort of psychic connection, a blending. Sometimes baby needs.

Belly/Abdomen: Often depicts being emotionally hurt. Also ability to 'digest' what you experience. Your hungers and longings.

Genitals: Usually to do with how you feel about your male or female sexuality, so men may dream of having a vagina when they meet their own feminine characteristics. Women might dream of having a penis when actively expressing their male nature.

Legs: Ability to stand up for yourself. Your psychological support and motivation. *Idioms*: Legless; Did not have a leg to stand on; My legs went to jelly; My legs were paralysed; I could not stand up for myself; Felt like I had a ball-and-chain on my legs.

Places — Environments

Places and environments range all the way from a warm holiday beach to a frightening mental hospital. By taking a moment to consider what feelings you attach to such places, you can usually arrive at an understanding of your dream. The beach scene, for instance, is an advertising cliché, suggesting a carefree and pleasurable time. Your use of such words is the best clue. Some examples are: 'I want to get away from it all into the country; he ought to be locked up in prison; like being at the factory; we spent the day on the beach.' Once again, do the mental exercise of translating such imagery into non-cliché everyday language.

Buildings — The range of different buildings is enormous, but they are usually fairly easy to decipher from their use. For example, a garage is obviously a place either to refuel or get your car repaired. In everyday language, the image depicts finding more energy/resources or getting yourself 'back on the road' again i.e. capable of working or being healthy.

Home — What do you mean by saying, 'I am homesick' or 'I want to get away from home'? Usually the feelings, attitudes and way of life you are used to or like. The situation, relationships and condition of home life, now or in the past. Like *House*, it can depict your body and mind.

House — A house is different to a home in that it may not be where you feel 'at home'. What the house means in your dream depends on its atmosphere and what is happening. A dark, dismal, lonely house obviously shows feelings of depression and loneliness. A house also may depict different parts of your body, feelings and mind. So *Basement*: Hidden memories and feelings. Connection with the powerful, instinctive urges and drives. *Kitchen*: Caring for yourself and others. Transformation. *Living/sitting-room*: Your personal 'space' to do things. Relaxation. *Toilet/Bathroom*: May depict both privacy or the need for it. The toilet is also a place of getting rid of tension, unwanted feelings or inner 'crap'. *Bathroom* is a change of feelings, a cleansing of down feelings or state of mind. *Bedroom*: Privacy. Relationship. Sex. Rest. *Attic/Loft*: Memories. The past. Somewhere to get away from everyday demands. An intellectual attitude. *Façade of house*: Public face. Social self.

Parts of a house are important, too. *Front door*: Attitudes to strangers. Who do you let into your life? *Back door*: The way you let family and friends into your life. *Windows*: Ability to be seen by or to see others. Your view of the world and others. *Stairs*: An obstacle or difficulty. Gaining or losing status or self-esteem. Skill in dealing with anxiety or challenge. *Garden*: Growth. Relaxation.

Hospital — Often depicts a healing process, or psychological or physical conditions needing attention.

Factory — It might point to issues connected with work, or a mechanistic outlook. A situation connected with economic rather than human needs.

Castle — Defensive attitudes or, conversely, a feeling of security. Old attitudes concerning conflict.

Church — Active or inherited attitudes to do with collective morals and beliefs. Feelings about the 'norm' in social beliefs, or concerning particular belief systems. Contact with the transcendent.
Hotel — Temporary situation. When do you use an hotel, and for what? Sometimes a passing affair. Or is it work?
School — What are your feelings about school and what did you learn there? Often to do with learning a lesson in life, or facing a test of some sort.
Gymnasium — An attempt or a need to get fit or to strengthen some aspect of yourself.
Places in building. Corridor/passage: Connections. No-man's-land, an in-between state. *Lift*: Rising excitement, position or sexuality, if going up. Sinking feeling, coming down to earth, losing esteem if descending. *Roof*: Protection from difficulties of life. If on the roof, may be a wider view of your situation. *Wall*: Restriction or protection. Attitudes or beliefs. Social restrictions. *Room*: If large, it depicts your possibilities, your mental 'space'. If small, the restrictions you feel around you or your limited mental view. *Plumbing*: How your emotions are dealt with or directed. Intestines or internal organs. *Electrical wiring*: Powerful, but sometimes dangerous drives, such as sex, ambition or the fear reaction.
Workplace — What do you feel about work? Usually points to your feelings concerning work, or work situation.

Elements: Weather and Nature

We often use weather and scenes to depict our moods. A relationship can be 'stormy', for instance, or someone's disposition 'sunny'. In trying to understand nature in your dreams, consider how you would use what appears in your dream if you were making a film. What mood or emotion might it portray? What aspect of your character or life would it illustrate?
Air: In dreams, air is usually what you are gasping for, or something you glide on in flight. In these cases, the gasping refers to feelings of anxiety or being in a stifling situation. The flight depends upon whether there is pleasure or 'flight' taking place. If 'flight', what are you or the thing/person flying escaping from? *Wind*: Hidden or unseen influences which move or even support you if flying on the wind. *Gale*: Dangerous emotions or events buffeting your confidence and good feelings.

Fire: Are you aware of what part fire plays in your life? See if you can define how you feel about the different ways it is used.

If the fire is pleasant: Feelings of warmth and comfort, even love. Sometimes represents homeliness. *If fire is dangerous*: Consuming emotions, such as anger or loss. Great change, often not easy. Warning that something needs attention. *Furnace or heater*: Emotional energy channelled for your own and other people's benefit. Strong sexual feelings — 'heat'. *Fire and water mixed*: A conflict or opposition, perhaps in relationship or work. *Lightning*: Intuition of sudden and possibly dramatic changes or problems. Tremendous emotional or sexual release, one you find threatening. *The sun*: Your transcendent self. Life energy. A life-giving influence. *Earth*: What is your relationship with the earth? Do you recognise your dependence? Physical life.

The past. The basic part of your life. Resources. *The world or a world*: The situation in which you live. Your 'world' of experience. *Hills or mountains*: If climbing, they represent your challenges or achievements, even difficulties. *Climbing* may sometimes depict the first half of life. If on top, it is a greater or wider perspective on your life. Achievement. *Going downhill* may refer to feelings of ease, losing status or ability, or old age. In women's dreams, it sometimes symbolises the menopause and the loss of a past way of life. *Rocks*: Strength. The eternal unchanging. The natural or spontaneous in your life. *Earthquakes*: enormous life changes. Sudden and shocking events.

Water: Think about the ways you relate to water and what each means. Consider these in connection with your dream.

Longing for a drink suggests a deep need for something, possibly emotional or sexual satisfaction. *River*: Emotions that can move or even drown you unless you deal with them well i.e. swim. Also a place of change such as (re)birth or death. *Sea*: Deep levels of consciousness below verbalisation, such as experienced in the womb and infancy. Intuitive levels of understanding. Storm at sea might show a release of unconscious feelings that could be felt as very threatening. A life change difficult to meet. *Lake*: Your inner feelings. For a woman it might represent the womb, the place within her from which a child emerges. *Rain*: Release of feelings, such as tears. Depressed feelings if an overcast situation.

Animals

Mammals — Do you like or fear animals? Can you identify with them and see traits you as a human still have? If possible, define what the animal is in yourself, for this helps to clarify how your dreams use them. Also remember the cultural caricatures you give them, such as the sly fox, the wise owl, etc.

Mammals often depict your more spontaneous reactions to circumstances. Your anger is often felt as anti-social, and your public sexuality might also be. But animals usually display these without your usual constraints, so you use them instead. Animals also depict your innate fear reactions, your sex drive, your quest for survival and reproduction. Therefore, when you dream of an animal, the question you need to ask yourself is whether you are overlooking some powerful activity in one or more of these basic drives. What the animal is doing tells you your interaction with whatever spontaneous feeling it is.

Animal with its young: Parental feelings. Your childhood experience of being parented. *Animal skin*: The instincts, traits, power or wisdom of the animal concerned. *Attacked by an animal*: Feeling threatened by your instincts or spontaneous feelings. *Baby animal*: A baby — sometimes connected with pregnancy. Yourself when young. Vulnerability and dependence. *Domestic animal*: Urges in yourself which you have learned to 'tame' or 'domesticate' with reasonable success. *Fear of animal*: Fear of your own or other people's unconstrained feelings and urges. *Female animals* or those with a *bump* might represent motherhood or pregnancy in women's dreams, or mothering in general. *Hiding from or trapped by an animal*: Feeling controlled or threatened by your own or other people's urges or emotions. *Neglect, mutilation or killing your 'animal'*: You have a responsibility to care for your animal drives, to see your emotional, sexual, nutritional and bodily needs are met. When this is not done, you have this sort of dream. *Pet*: Feelings to do with dependence or being 'kept' by someone. May also depict feelings of pleasure or affection if it is a pet cat or dog. These are often sources of affection, so can represent caring for someone or need for love. Children sometimes have pet dreams as they are trying to grow out of dependence.

When looking at such dreams, remember the hundreds of ways animals are used in language — 'She's a bitch', 'He's like an animal', 'Sick as a dog', 'Weasel-faced', 'Bull in a china shop', etc.

Fish — In your dreams, you often use fish to depict what is going on under the surface in your body and mind, so catching a fish can refer to getting a new idea or realising an intuition. But fish can also represent hidden body processes. In a woman's dream, small fish in a container could show what is happening in her womb, an intuition of pregnancy, for instance. In a man, this might refer to sperm and male sexuality. Fish may also link with idioms you use, such as 'Cold fish', 'Fish out of water' or 'Slippery fish'.

Birds — These have an extremely wide number of possible meanings. Because of their flight, birds can represent your mind, imagination, soaring feelings and intuition. Their ability to have a 'bird's-eye view' of the world means you may use them to depict your capacity to have an overall picture of events or situations. The fact that you can often witness their growth and struggle to leave and survive the nest means they can symbolise your effort to become independent or to 'nest-build' and become a parent. Freud said a bird represented the sexual organs, and flying the sex act. In some languages the word 'bird' means woman, in others penis.

> **BIRD DREAM**
>
> 'An old lady made room for me to sit at the end of one of the three seats of a bus. As we drove away, a very large chicken-size baby bird flew in.
>
> 'It had short, stubby wings and yellow down, but flew expertly. I believe it first landed on the lady, and chirped squeakily. But in its squeaks it actually spoke, saying it had lost its mother. It sounded as if it were crying' — Andrew.

Different types of bird can mean various things. *Black birds* are often synonymous with death or despair because of their carrion habits. *Baby bird*, as in the box, links with childhood. Andrew felt abandoned by his mother: his dream shows he is still deeply affected by this. A *vulture* suggests waiting for gain from someone else's loss. An *owl* depicts seeing beyond the obvious, or intuition. Bird idioms are 'Free as a bird,' 'Wise old owl', 'A bird' — meaning a woman — 'A bird told me', 'Bird has flown', 'Bird in the hand', 'Bird of ill-omen' and 'Odd bird'.

Reptiles and Snakes — As explained earlier, one of the three levels of your brain, the medulla, has been called 'the lizard brain'. Neuroscientist Paul MacLean says we have three brains, the most primitive being the medulla. This part still deals with the same functions it did in the lizard, namely flight and fight, reproduction, territory and ritual behaviour.

I believe a lizard or snake in dreams shows what is happening at this very basic — but crucially important — level of your consciousness. This is why snakes and lizards are so often linked with sex. But they represent much more than that. They are also the wonder of the instinctive life in you trying forever to move towards survival, even if blindly. The snake and lizard symbolise the sexual, emotional and mental energy within. Like electricity, this energy is able to accomplish almost anything. In the home, it can power a light, produce music, TV images, heat us or kill us.

> ### SNAKES
>
> 'I came across a lot of snakes and they swarmed onto me. I froze, terrified that if I made a move I would be fatally bitten. But they just swarmed over my body and got under my clothes without harming me. Gradually, I relaxed and slowly began to move about with the snakes still on me. They started to feel like a built-in defence system' — Des.
>
> Des explored the dream and discovered the snakes were his repressed aggression and masculine power. He was learning to release this in a non-destructive way.

Your 'snake' energy may produce illness — through being expressed as fear or terrible depression — or become amazing mental creativity and emotional pleasure, depending on how you relate to it. What is happening to the snake/lizard in your dreams shows what you are doing with your creative/destructive energy. Therefore, being bitten by a snake depicts the emotional energy turned against yourself or someone else.

Plants — Trees

Define your feelings about plants and trees, for this will give you insight into dreams about them.

In general, any plant, tree, flower, shrub, etc, depicts the process of change, growth and survival. The situation in which plants or flowers appear comments upon how well or badly the growth or unfolding of personal qualities is occurring. But flowers and plants have many other associations. Giving flowers depicts a sharing or expression of tender feelings or love. The flowers may also connect with special times, such as weddings, birthdays and funerals, showing emotions associated with such events. Tending plants illustrates an attempt at nurturing some new thing in your life, or caring for the growth of other people.

Fruit — What is nourishing to you, or a reward for your labours or endeavour. This is a sort of cause-and-effect symbol, a 'What you sow, so shall you reap' image. Therefore, the quality of the fruit is important, showing how satisfied you are with your lot. Particular fruits have special meanings, like the *apple*, sometimes depicting temptation in relationships, at other times a breast. *Pomegranate* denotes female sexuality and fertility, and *banana* a male penis.

Vegetables — Basic physical needs and rewards.

Trees — These are enormously potent symbols of your whole life and the stages of growth through which you go, and the many branches you develop in different skills and various relationships. The trunk and roots may show links with ancestors and society — the family tree — whilst the branches and seeds point to children. The stages of growth the tree goes through and the seasons it weathers are also indicators of your life, with the sapling referring to youth and a mature tree to middle years. The spring leaves denote youth and vigour whereas summer is the mature years. The autumn leaves and bare branches of winter refer to old age.

> **DIANA AND THE TREE**
>
> 'When I was eight years old, I dreamt I was sitting in a large garden with my family and a baby boy. We climbed a big tree, the baby as well, to see what was at the top. The baby fell out of the tree and seemed to be asleep. Then the baby had gone. In its place was a bluebird that flew away' — Diana.
>
> In her dream, Diana not only explores what she might grow into as an adult, but also looks at death — the loss of the baby.

Objects

Objects in dreams very much reflect the feelings and value you place upon them and what function they play in your life. A ring might represent a relationship while a pen is something with which to express thoughts. Although objects, such as a car or money, have a general social connection, they often hold very personal associations, too.

You might have been given the wrist-watch in the dream by your father. It could be you therefore treasure it or have difficult feelings because of bad relationship memories, so consider such points when looking for insight into objects in a dream. If possible, write down your associations. Then, for the general associations, ask yourself: 'What do I feel about this thing? How do I use it? What does it add or take away from my life? What is the context of the object in the dream saying about it?'

> I found that although I had plenty of money — coins — each time I went to pay for something, I discovered the coins were all tied together with something rather like spider's web thread, which made it impossible to untangle — Miss J. B.

In this example, the money would play quite a different role if it were not tied together. Without the threads, it suggests being rich. With them, it indicates difficulty about spending or aspects to 'untangle' regarding money or getting her needs.

Food and Drink — Questions to ask are, 'For what are you hungering?' 'Does this refer to your health needs?' and 'Is this a compensation for something else?'

In general, food usually refers to needs and energy, your longing and social position — whether you can get enough to eat.

Money — This concerns what you value, what you give and what you hold on to. In dreams, money will sometimes also refer to your self-esteem, or lack of it, and what power you feel in society. See box.

Tools — Usually refers to their function. A spade would suggest we are digging for something, such as information or insight. In general, they represent skills or mental tools we use.

AMANDA'S MONEY

'I was aware of having a lot of money in a night safe that I had to hide from somebody who was coming to steal it. I knew he would look in the usual hiding place so found a secret compartment in the mattress. But when I put it in, it looked so obvious I was afraid he would notice when he made the bed' — Amanda.

Amanda is obviously frightened something she values will be taken from her by a male.

Clothes — What do clothes mean to you? What feelings do they provoke? How much do you depend on them for your self-esteem? Clothes often depict the feelings and attitudes you adopt or cover yourself in socially or even privately. Clothing can so alter appearance you are able to present yourself as anything from a tramp to a princess. Dream clothes will therefore illustrate how you are feeling and want to be seen. The following dream from H shows this:

> Looking in a mirror, I saw I had on stockings and a suspender belt, with a very short, frilly petticoat. It looked very sexy. I was aware the door was open and had an urge to close it, but then felt OK about looking sexy and people seeing me.

Clothes may also be a form of protection or sign of a role, like wearing armour or a soldier's uniform. Being without clothes is usually either a sign of feeling very exposed or vulnerable, or of wanting people to notice us and perhaps be sexually attracted.

Musical instruments — Self-expression. Creativity. Sexual matters. The music produced is an expression of emotions and shades of feeling.

Machines — Often the actions we perform mechanically or habitually. A machine may well refer to the automatic functions of your body so might represent the pumping of your heart.

Transport

Most of us have quite a different attitude to a personally owned car than we do to public transport or riding in a lorry. Ask yourself what feelings you have about your dream transport.

Car: Independence. Ability to work. Status in some way. Also your ability to choose a direction, your sex 'drive' and capacity to deal with other people on the highway of life. The ability to include others in where you want to go.

Sitting at the *driving wheel* shows you directing your life. Being a *passenger* suggests going along with someone else. A *breakdown* shows you feeling you are not getting anywhere or there is a problem in work, a relationship, etc. Idioms: 'Back seat driver', 'Drive at', 'Drive away', 'Drive somebody mad/round the bend/round the twist/to drink', 'What are you driving at?', 'Taking someone/being taken for a ride'.

Bus: Your direction and connection with other people.

Train: A set direction, therefore something like work where you are with others going along in a particular way. Train of events set in motion.

Lorry/Truck: Similar to car, but connected more with commercial ventures. Big events, like moving or work.

Plane: Rapid change of life situation. Plans, hopes, loves that are 'up in the air', so may end as hoped, but might crash. Ambitious endeavours. An aeroplane attacking suggests anxiety from which it is difficult to escape. The ability to get away.

Boat/Ship: Often concerns a relation-'ship' of some form. It is difficult to get out of a ship and go your own way, so suggests contracts with people, such as marriage. The ship and boat also show how you deal with the stormy seas and calm waters of life's journey.

Light and Shade

When it is light and sunny in a dream, it usually depicts feelings of positive happiness. Light also means we are aware of circumstances, events, our environment, etc. We can 'see' in the light. In the dark we are less able to move easily and less confident. Some nightmares centre around not being able to put on the light and dispel fear, so the *dark* can point to feelings of fear, of not being aware, a sense of evil or the unknown.

Time — Seasons

An idea of how you use time and seasons in your life can be gained by remembering such sayings as 'It was too late', 'I did not have time', 'The autumn of life', 'Like a spring lamb', etc.

In general, *time* refers to feelings about satisfying yourself with what you have achieved, or the time of your life i.e. *midday* might refer to mid-life or the active working period and the *evening* the 'evening' of life, or the period of relaxation. *Night* has many associations. These range from rest, relaxation and freedom from work, through depression or a difficult period in life to finding one's unconscious inner life, the events that take place in the dark; sexual encounter.

Spring suggests birth or a new beginning. *Summer* a time of fulfilment, relaxation, warmth and pleasure. *Autumn* middle or old age, fruition and rewards of activity, decline. *Winter* the end, a time to wait or not start new projects.

Temperature

Temperature is used in everyday speech to suggest how you are reacting to people or situations e.g. 'He was too hot to handle', 'The goods were hot', 'He was as cold as a fish', 'The scent had gone cold', 'He has a really warm personality', etc.

Temperature in dreams is exactly along those lines. Cold or ice usually refer to frozen emotions or feeling cold about somebody. Hot indicates strong feelings moving towards sex, anger or passion of some kind. For fuller information on dream symbols see *The New Dream Dictionary*.[50]

6
Destiny and Dreams

The inner world of dreams has similarities to your external world. Most of us have some idea of what and where Africa is. If we travelled in the right direction, we should reach Africa. It would have similarities with what other people found, but still be a uniquely personal experience.

Your psyche or mind also has a geography. If you travel long enough in its domain you will meet certain 'countries' of the mind. Lots of people have been to these lands — or in some cases even live there — but your experience will be unique. To understand your dreams, it helps if you have an introduction to some of these great countries. It will also help if you have a concept of human personality that fits with exploring your dreams.

The Tree of Life
In the imagery of dreams a tree is often used to depict a person's growth from conception through birth to old age and death. This extraordinary process of growth is not the result of your personal will or wisdom. It happens despite your intentions.

Marie von Franz, writing in Jung's book *Man and His Symbols*,[51] says: 'The fact that we often speak of "arrested development" shows that we assume that such a process of growth and maturation is possible with every individual. Since this psychic growth cannot be brought about by a conscious effort of will power, but happens involuntarily and naturally, it is in dreams frequently symbolised by the tree, whose slow, powerful, involuntary growth fulfils a definite pattern.'

Recognising this spontaneous process of growth is important when looking at dreams. This growth does not stop with physical maturity, but continues throughout your lifetime. It underlies both physical and psychological change. It pervades every aspect of your life, and therefore every aspect of your dream life. That it is not an expression of your will means it is self-regulating. It orders and directs its own processes. But when you recognise it and work with your dreams, you blend your creativity and courage with its power. Then consciousness and the unconscious work together in the creative art of life.

This is like the art of the gardener. But your personality and dreams are not completely unconscious processes. Because you have self-awareness, the strange, wonderful fact of consciousness shines a light back into the deepest recesses of your being. What might have been a completely unconscious 'natural' activity becomes to some extent conscious, intelligent and directed. Your dreams are certainly highly intelligent comment on your life. The following dream from Zack illustrates this:

> I was in a large cellar, finishing cleaning it. There had been a good deal of rubbish in it, but it was now clean and painted white, with a lot of space. When I explored the dream, I realised it was the space inside myself I had cleared. There had been many difficulties in my marriage, and I had the sense of having dealt with them. I then imagined carrying the dream forward and walked upstairs. Above the cellar was a lovely cottage. My wife was there. I felt such love for her, and a sense that I could at last be the husband I wanted.

Through his dream, Zack discovered that he had made real changes in his life, so it confirmed and strengthened his conscious action. The analogy of the tree in the sort of personal growth he achieved can be usefully extended. The tree does not spring into being from nowhere. The seed from which it grew carries ancient ancestry. It contains all the past experience of its forebears, but faces a unique situation in its place of growth, soil condition and climate, and the bacterial, insect and animal attacks with which it might have to deal. The tree therefore carries the past into the present, but it also holds in itself the possibilities of what it might become in the face of its environment.

In approaching dreams, you need to remember that you cannot control the most profound of your life processes. The power that grows you is spontaneous and self-regulating. You can work with it or ignore it. You can fight it. But you cannot control it. This power of growth holds in it all that you have been and all that you might be. It is all your ancestry and future. It has great wisdom, but is unconscious until you throw light on it. This power is one of the 'countries' of the dream.

Geography of Dreams
The continents and lands of your dreams, the oceans to traverse and dive into, are all evident in the dream themes and the life facts each of us meets. We all experience growth and ageing. We nearly all encounter some level of sexual drive. We face or run from the need to become a member of society. We all confront death, indirectly and directly. The names of the lands we travel in dreams are Infancy, Childhood, Adolescence, Maturity, To Be or Not To Be, Ageing and Death. The oceans are called Demands of External Reality and Norms, Demands of Internal Reality and Drives, Mind, Trauma, Independence and Transcendence.

There are also dwellers in the lands of dream. These are the men and women, children and babies, animals, trees and plants that people your dreams. To live in the land of dreams with any sort of peace or pleasure you will need to develop a relationship with the inhabitants of your dream lands. In essence, these inhabitants are the aspects of yourself you are not well enough acquainted with in waking life, or have business to deal with. They are parts of you that have become in some degree disconnected or even split off from your waking personality, from the main sense of yourself.

As an example, you may not be able to remember your childhood or babyhood in any detail. Can you recall what it was like to live in the eternal before you developed a concept and experience of time? Can you recollect life before speech? Have you experienced the enormous passion and power of your dependence upon parents or carers? Many people have no real recollection of their childhood. Therefore, this part of their life is split off. It is not integrated with their adult view of the world and the decisions they make. It does not figure, except perhaps in a negative way, in dealings with their own or other people's children and babies. To be a whole person, you will need to meet your baby, to make friends with your child, to integrate your animal and develop a working relationship with the other non-dominant parts of yourself.

The most common dreams are about how you meet and effectively deal with these inhabitants of your dreams, with the ordinary and extraordinary human dilemmas and facts you face. Jung said that if you reach middle age, you encounter what he called 'individuation'. But from birth onwards you face the process of separation, and it continues to haunt you unless you deal with it creatively. Dreams constantly return to this theme of becoming an individual. But at the same time they paradoxically deal with how you as an individual can be more in harmony with the Whole of which you are a part, and the parts that make you a whole.

Your Most Frequent Dreams
During my many hours of radio phone-ins about dreams, those most frequently mentioned were recurring and anxiety dreams. It is not true to say these are the most common dreams generally, but they are often the most memorable.

Anxiety or fear are a natural part of life for the majority of animals. Through sharply honed awareness, fear enables animals and humans to survive difficult environments. However, as a self-aware human you face something animals do not. Because you have language and can create imaginative scenes, you are able to think about fear-producing situations and make yourself anxious outside a real situation. You might falsely suspect your partner of having an affair. The false anxiety is just as painful as the true one. In the mind of imagination whatever you believe to be true is true as far as your feeling reaction is concerned. Just imagining you will not be able to pay your next electricity bill can produce profound anxiety. To deal with it many humans smoke, drink or use drugs to allay the sharp prod of fear. But there are other ways to meet it. Our dreams help us achieve a growth that changes our relationship with fear.

Nightmares
An example of anxiety in dreams is that during a nightmare you totally believe the awful situation to be true. When you wake, you can say to yourself, 'This is just a dream.' This thought enables you to drop your belief in the dream's reality. Although this is fairly obvious, it is an important point when dealing with anxiety in

dreams or waking. In the following example, the dreamer is totally immersed in the dream's reality. Abe R said:

> Dreamt I was alone in a house and asleep in bed. Something materialised or landed at the foot of the bed. It woke me a little and I felt afraid. I had the feeling it was some sort of entity materialising and coming for me. It moved up the bed. I felt paralysed, partly by fear, but also as if the 'thing' was influencing me. This made me more afraid of it. Then it moved up higher. I was very afraid and struggling against the paralysing influence. I managed to shout at it: 'I will destroy you! I will destroy you!' As I shouted, I pushed at it with my hand. This felt to me as if I wanted to will its destruction and use my hand to smash it. At this point I woke. My wife told me I had been pushing her and shouting that I would destroy her.

Abe was in his early fifties at the time of the dream. The ageing process had suddenly galloped along and was apparent on his body. In his own words:

> Recently, it is obvious from the mirror that my body is going through another period of rapid ageing. In the dream, death is gradually creeping up on me, gradually overwhelming me, and I am fighting it. I explored these feelings by working on the dream images. I realised I felt death had put its finger on me. The touch of death was like a disease. Once touched, ageing gradually takes over your body and is incurable. I could hardly breathe as I experienced this. I understood the sort of emotions which might lie beneath asthma attacks. This struggle with death went on for some time. It was not terrible, but was felt strongly.

Abe's dream is a typical nightmare. If he had not been someone who explores his dreams, Abe would perhaps have got on with everyday life, looking back on the nightmare as a complete but frightening mystery. For most people, that is where it ends. But Abe took it steps further by exploring his dream. He uncovered the deeply felt anxiety underlying the images. Now he could see for himself that he had much more anxiety about ageing than he had ever admitted to himself. But the imagery of dreams allowed him not simply to find out what fears he felt, but to discover a different relationship with them. If Abe had stopped at the point where he realised the extent of his fear, he might have ended by saying, 'I'm really scared of ageing.' However, Abe is an old hand with dreams and the feelings they uncover, so went a step further. He describes this as follows:

> Feeling so scared was not a good place to be. So I wanted to face the truth about death, whatever it was. I wanted to walk right up to it and look it in the face and know whether death meant a final end. If it did, I would rather know. I would rather face it now and get the fear over with than have it put a cloud over my life. So I imagined walking up to the thing at the bottom of the bed. As I approached it, my feelings went through an amazing transformation. All the tension left me. I felt good, positive and with a sense of hope about life and death. This was so surprising and sudden I wondered what had produced it. I needed to be aware of how this change had occurred so I could use it in my life.
>
> I retraced my steps to look at death and try to understand why it had lost its power to frighten. I remembered that someone said on TV a few days previously, 'Life is a sexually transmitted disease which produces one hundred per cent mortality.' Seen in this way, death is the rotting corpse, the skeleton. The path to it is disease or breakdown. Those were the thoughts that scared me.
>
> But in looking death in the face, I saw another view of it. I saw the dead body, the corpse and the skeleton as forms left behind by the process of life, like a snail leaves a shell. When I looked at myself to see what 'Abe' is, I cannot separate myself from the process of life. The deeper I dig into myself, the fuller I see that I and the process of life are one. That process leaves behind shells, bodies and tree trunks, but it goes on creating other forms. With sudden wonder, I realised that I could either identify with my body or Life. My fear then disappeared and has not returned.

Abe's nightmare and his exploration demonstrate clearly how ideas — in this case his concept of death — create anxiety. But his words also show how, by accepting that each of us has a potential for dealing with a problem, you can find your way through it. In virtually every anxiety dream, by having the courage to walk up and 'look it in the face' this transformation can occur. If that is not your style, if you cannot walk up to your own emotions and face them, at least remember what was said about reality earlier in the book.

- There is no such thing as objectivity. We cannot eliminate ourselves from the universe. It and we are not separate. Everybody and everything has a point of view.
- We are participators. The universe in some strange way may be brought into being by our participation.

This means that our concept of what is real actually creates that reality in some degree. Therefore, there is no set reality. If our view of 'reality' is not what we want, we can shift to another 'viewpoint' as Abe did.

Recurring Dreams

Recurring dreams are intriguing or sometimes troubling. The most extreme case I have on record is of a woman who had exactly the same dream every night. Even though that is almost unique, most of us either have a dream that repeats a few times or a recurring theme, sometimes with a gap of a year or years. The following dream illustrates some of the key features of such dreams:

> Years ago, I lost my first husband at twenty-nine. I had the same dream continually of being in a phone box trying to contact him, not understanding why he had left me. He died of cancer. Later, I remarried and this husband died of a heart attack. Once again the same dream came back so much — Mrs C. J.

Common sense tells us why Mrs J has this dream time after time. It is because the difficult emotions — and the questions about why it should happen — are powerfully active in her. But as she almost certainly knew these things troubled her, why should she keep having the dream? The answer is almost as commonplace as the reason for her dreams. With something that is deeply important, most of us repeat our attempts to succeed if we do not immediately achieve what we seek. Mrs J was attempting two important tasks.

Firstly, she was trying to come to terms with what happened and the feelings with which it left her. Secondly, she was attempting to understand why it occurred, particularly after the second time. The self-regulatory process in dreams tries to resolve anything that is blocking a reasonably balanced response to life. It seeks to find answers to important questions. It tries to help us continue our psychological growth and clear up issues, even if they are years old.

Unless you bring conscious attention to what it is doing, it is, in part, a blindly instinctive force, like a river trying to find its way through the debris of your hurts and confusions. The nightmare Abe explored shows this. His attention helped the nightmare 'unblock' and move on to satisfying attitudes. Mrs J did not explore her dream. There is every likelihood that it repeated itself because there was some aspect of her feelings about her husband she had not felt or recognised.

There is, of course, also the aspect of recurring dreams dealing with practising a situation, or meeting a feeling again and again until you find a different relationship with it. This is seen in dreams that are recurring, but evolve. They gradually shift from being frustrating or frightening to a resolution. An interesting dream depicting this is one that many of us had as children if we lived in a house with stairs. The dream usually starts with us trying to run downstairs, but there is anxiety about falling or stumbling. As the dream recurs, we gradually get better at going fast down the stairs. The final 'satisfying' end to the recurring series is often as follows:

> I have the sensation of skimming down a long flight of stairs, sometimes straight, frequently with a bend. I seem to slide on my toes at great speed, like a tea-tray going down and around corners with a great leap, four stairs or so at a time. Very exhilarating! — Joan Pinker.

The explanation for the series is possibly that, as children, stairs are difficult to climb, and even harder to descend. There is very real danger involved. Therefore, as you practise coming down the stairs in dreams, you are gradually achieving the mastery of fear and the physical skill of descent. When you finally manage to do so easily and fast, it is like flying and you have the exhilaration of mastering what was frightening.

Most recurring dreams fit into these two categories (a) The attempt to deal with a past trauma or a current deeply felt issue (b) Practising a social or physical skill, or exploring a question in an attempt to resolve it. To help the dream get out of its stuck loop, use the technique described in Chapter Four under the heading of *Acting In*, and the sub-heading *And Then What?* This is where you continue the dream in imagination to some sort of satisfying conclusion.

The Psychological Dream

The psychological dream is the most frequent of all the many types we experience. What have already been described as the 'anxiety dream' and the 'recurring dream' are really both psychological dreams. This is also true of many dreams often called 'precognitive' or to do with someone else. Because you may fail to see how your dreams use the image of someone else to portray your own attitudes or talents, you might say, 'Oh, I dreamt about Teddy the other day', and really believe the dream concerned him.

When I was teaching in Iceland, virtually everyone to whom I spoke believed that most of their dreams predicted future events. This was because their cultural view of dreams is that they are predictive psychic events. Witnessing hundreds of people exploring their dreams in the way suggested already had assured me that most of the time we are dealing with our own past as it expresses in our present difficulties, relationships, fears and buried trauma.

You are the great theme of your dreams. **You** are the mystery your dreams explore and reveal. As you will gradually discover if you take the journey into yourself, you are much more than you thought. You are not simply a person who was born to certain people and now lives in a particular country. The threads that are woven together to form you are drawn from ancient times. Your attitudes, language, thoughts and responses are inherited from great and ignoble people who lived long ago. Perhaps you will modify those impulses and concepts. Possibly you will add to them. But your life does not escape them.

The tree of your life has its roots not just in the genetic material passed to you by your parents. You arose not only from a gene pool, but also a behavioural pool and a language/concept pool. Ask yourself which of your concepts, words, habits or responses are unique to you. If you did not create them out of the void, where did they come from? Are these inherited aspects of yourself you? Do you identify with them completely? Or is the fundamental 'you' something which takes on and uses them, and can perhaps change?

Some of the first aspects you meet in psychological dreams are your baby, your child, and your adolescent, all of whom need to be not only met but perhaps re-experienced. In your task of integrating them, it is not enough to get to know them intellectually and develop friendly dialogue. They demand to be loved, to be fully taken into your life as if absorbing them into your whole being. This means experiencing what it was like to be the baby afraid of being abandoned, what it was like to feel so tremendously afraid, angry or totally lost.

The good old, common, everyday psychological dream constantly looks at and plays with these enormously important themes. They are the big issues of your life.

On Your Own

Birth is possibly the most primal and powerful experience any of us ever face. Culturally, we are conditioned to believe that we do not remember it. However, there are too many dreams and sessions of exploration that lead back to it for us seriously to believe we forget. Out of the minutes, the hours, the eternity of our birth struggle patterns of behaviour evolve that colour the rest of our life.

Birth has many aspects. There is the possible trauma of birth or pre-maturity, but there is also the wonder of emergence, or rebirth because of the new beginning. After all, conception was also a beginning. Along with birth come the enormous new experiences we meet through the attempt to bond with our mother/carer, and the associated feelings of dependence and vulnerability. Something else that connects with birth that exists in us as children but may be lost as adults is the continual wonder as to where we came from.

Birth dreams might include being trapped; fighting through a tunnel or trying to get out of a hole; being tortured; the Devil, hell and/or heaven; feeling overwhelmed; being strangled; underwater and not breathing, or not needing to breathe; being born deformed. For further information read *Different Doorway: Adventures of a Caesarian Born*. This book is by Jane English, a physicist who writes about her dreams and how they helped uncover the influence of a Caesarian birth in her life. Stanislav Grof's book, *Realms of The Human Unconscious*, is also recommended.

Separation and its accompanying move to independence are not limited to birth and childhood. They are lifelong challenges. We meet them in the leaving of parents, losing a job and the death or parting of a partner. Being out of work for a long period is a huge experience of separation. During it we face feelings of enormous aloneness that force us to recognise how much connection with our social group we felt through work.

Having self-awareness is a contributor to loneliness and feelings of separation. The story of the Garden of Eden is about birth and its challenge of separation. In the Garden, we were at-one with everything — and are then cast out of this at-one-ment into becoming an individual. This separation from God is the original state of oneness which was felt before we developed self-awareness, guided by instinct or intuition. Erich Fromm sees this as a historical process, deepening with the period of the Renaissance and Reformation.[52]

> **POSSIBLE BIRTH DREAMS**
>
> 'My five-year-old son has two recurring dreams. In them, I either kick him down the stairs, or two men come to kill him. He has been telling me these dreams ever since he could talk. They upset me as I cannot think of anything that has happened to make him fear me'— Karon.
>
> Karon had a long and difficult delivery lasting 28 hours.
>
> 'I am being forced swiftly through a dark, very narrow tunnel. I feel pain as I am dragged along, and hear loud banging noises which frighten me. Although they are loud, they seem to come from inside my head. I feel terrified and breathless, and very relieved when I wake before reaching the end of the tunnel. In fact, as I write this account I am shivering.

This confrontation with being an individual who is no longer an integral part of a family or social group — and possibly not even connected in the way of marriage or work — is quite new historically. People were made outlaws from their tribe or religion in the past, but not in such numbers or so subtly as in today's world. Therefore, there is no great highway of behaviour set out for us by parents, or easily accessible role models. This really is dream territory where we wrestle with all that is and confronts us to arrive at a new way of being that satisfies.

Writing about this sort of situation, Jung says: '. . . I had learned to see that the greatest and most important problems of life are all fundamentally insoluble. They must be so, because they express the necessary polarity inherent in every self-regulating system. They cannot be solved, but only outgrown. I therefore asked myself whether this possibility of outgrowing, or further psychic development, was not normal, while to remain caught in a conflict was something pathological.'[53]

Finding your way to real independence that is not at odds with society or yourself isn't easy. Jung named it 'individuation'. It is a creative act because you re-form your whole being in some measure. If you succeed, you emerge from the death of your past. You rise from ashes. You meet challenges and conflicts that cannot be faced without courage and resources. Your inner life of dreams is the greatest guide on this journey. Only it can respond to the unplanned, unfamiliar way, creating a path out of the emptiness of the unknown.

The Struggle with Opposites

Our existence is a paradox of extreme opposites. The life process that we are has existed since the dawn of time. In a sense our body is the latest leaf on a tree millions of years old, yet we constantly face the ending of things and death. Waking and sleeping are extremes of experience. Infancy and age are two other polarities. Even within ourselves we face the extremes of focused self-awareness while awake and the void of unconsciousness when we sleep or relax deeply.

These extremes are expressed in our dreams in a number of ways. The polarities of consciousness reveal themselves in a meeting with the transcendent with its awareness of eternal life, at the same time facing death and the grave. This polarity may also be met as an experience of samadhi/nirvana/the womb of blissful existence, and its opposite in death-pits of despair about the futility of life.

There is a delicate balancing act within us between the opposites of male and female. Our mind has many divisions, either because of its functioning or due to trauma that split us. Love, or the need for it, can also cause many divisions in us. Our childhood need for a bonded relationship is so intense it can be at the root of enormous opposites within us. When this need is hurt we can leave behind the developing personality we were and take an entirely new path of development. The following dream shows this:

> I am alone in a street somewhere in the city of London. I am standing looking at a nearby old-fashioned phone box. It is a weekend when all is quiet. The door of the phone box is open, and on the floor is a variety of bones. At first I think they are animal, but quickly see they are human. Then a man enters the box to make a call. Suddenly, three or four savage dogs attack, ripping him to pieces — Sam.

The background to Sam's dream — and what he experienced when he explored it — is that he was put into an orphanage as a small child. Sam was not, in fact, an orphan. His father was an alcoholic, and his mother felt she could no longer care for Sam. However, she kept some of his siblings at home with her. Sam spent years in the orphanage before being taken home again. He describes what he found in exploring his dream as follows:

> One of the first things I noticed was a knotted feeling in my stomach. When I wondered what this knotted lump was, I experienced a picture in my mind of a lump that I had kept deep within me that no one could touch, or ever has done. I split the lump to see what was inside. There appeared two halves of a walnut, with a picture of my mother in one half and father in the other, as they were when I was a child. The secret I had carried since childhood was that unlike other children in the orphanage, I had parents. Yet the truth was that I, too, had been left.
>
> The emotions now came to the surface and I really cried about being left and wanting my mother. The dream was depicting this loneliness in the orphanage. But it also held the loneliness I later felt when living once more with my parents in and around the City of London. This was why the dream showed me standing alone in the City.
>
> After this wave of emotion and insight passed, I was left in a very passive state. I imagined myself in the telephone box trying to make a call. The need for the call arose from my tremendous sense of isolation and abandonment. This had haunted me right from childhood through into adult life. In the image of the man making a call, I was trying to reconnect, to assure myself that I was loved. The dream was so precise in that the call was being

made from a lonely place, and an abandoned feeling in myself.

Again another shock — there was nobody with whom to connect. Nobody was on the end of the line. I had never before really admitted to myself that I was alone, that I had been abandoned in the orphanage. I had always lived in the hope that someone actually wanted me. With the realisation that I was an orphan, another great wave of emotion tore through me.

When the emotions subsided, I turned towards the dogs as they came at me. I began to feel the sickness that I have experienced for years when feeling alone. But I just shrugged and let the feeling wash over me. I could see I have always ended up in hell by that route, and realised that the hell I feel in having been abandoned will never be anything else. I could feel the dogs' attack as the anxieties that have torn me apart for years, anxieties about relationship and whether I am loved. I could see from these feelings that the dogs of my anxieties have consumed two-thirds of my energy, two-thirds of my life, constantly tearing me apart. I also saw that as a kid I did not have enough information to re-direct the energy elsewhere.

This simple but powerful dream shows the level after level of feeling and memories that can be linked with apparently straightforward imagery. It illustrates how a dream is psychological, dealing with present life situation as it emerges from past experience. It also graphically shows how splits can occur and what they mean. Sam's dogs are not something apart from him. They are his own emotions that turn back and tear him apart. They turn on him because they are his doubts about being loved, his own need, and his own anger.

The polarities, paradoxes and splits in our nature cannot usually be dealt with by a simplistic approach. As with the new physics, none of us can avoid having a viewpoint. But this means there are many viewpoints, each looking at the world and arriving at our own truth. Is there an absolute truth or goal? In your dream life, aiming only at the one polarity of your being is to negate another side of yourself and cause unbalance.

The way towards resolution may be between the opposites, as P. W. Martin suggests in *Experiment in Depth*.[54] Sam says that being torn apart had consumed two-thirds of his energy, two-thirds of his life. Finding the way between the opposites and healing the hurt of trauma releases great floods of new energy. Caldwell describes this by saying: 'With the healing of a psychic wound or the relief of a galling fear, there comes a sudden access of glorious sweetness and joy. Light fills the consciousness, a light which is the essence of all happiness: incense and melody to the senses, understanding and triumph to the heart.' This is what wholeness means. And wholeness is an integrity of our opposites.

Sexual Connections

As a baby the distinction between hunger and sexual response does not exist. Breast feeding and sexual pleasure are interwoven. Even in adults the female breast and sexual pleasure are still intertwined. This lack of distinction means that as babies we have deep sexual feelings when we experience feeding satisfaction. Simultaneously, we embark upon a loving relationship, and at the same time have sensory stimulus. Therefore, sex and the development of personality are very much connected.

Like any other fundamental drive, our sexual responses can be hurt, twisted or expressed in an extraordinary number of ways. This fundamental power of our sex instinct can be manipulated and directed by external pressures such as advertising, and political, religious and social rules or taboos. Whoever controls or directs our sexual energy has their hands on our money, direction and soul. Therefore, our sexual dreams might feature childhood experience of sex and how we are hurt or conditioned as we age. They may be an attempt to find our own place in the social, economic, religious and political climate of our environment or what is happening in our present circumstances and relationship. They can also be a time of enormous release and pleasure.

There are too many issues connected with sex to be dealt with here. Everything from establishing one's sexual identity as a man or woman, to the incest question, spiritual guilt and anxiety might be met in your journey toward sexual wholeness. I went through years of misery in connection with sex, so know from personal experience that such chronic distress can be wiped away through the self-understanding and change dreamwork can bring.

This was achieved with the help of other ordinary men and women, not professional therapists. If, like myself in those years, you are economically limited in the help you can seek, do not give up. Use the techniques described in the previous chapters. Practise them until you become skilled. Gather information from wherever you can. Break free of your pain and confusion! Escape from the many authorities and powers that try to make you into their supporter or means of income.

Sexual dreams manifest in disguise: they come direct, appearing as beauty and the beast. It all depends upon your relationship with your needs and body. Here is a very direct sexual dream:

> I was in a building with a number of people. A woman I worked with many years ago was there, sitting cross-legged on the floor. I went and kissed her. She responded and I put my hand down on her thigh under her skirt, and gently moved under her knickers to touch her vagina. It was moist and wet with excitement. I pushed my fingers into the slippery crevice. As I did so, my feelings rose in a beautiful soft and satisfying orgasm. I thought I had ejaculated, but hadn't.
>
> Then I was in a street and met a dark-haired young woman. We embraced and kissed. The feeling of mutual pleasure was intense, so much so I felt what she was feeling, as if we did not have separate bodies. I felt an orgasm grow inside her pelvis and reach its pitch, flowing into the rest of her body. It was her orgasm, but it felt as if it were also mine. It was a beautiful, melting experience with no harshness or disappointment anywhere — Pete.

Pete's dream is obviously one in which his sexual feelings are easily and pleasurably allowed. This next example is one in which sex is hidden in symbols. This is a classic Freudian-type dream, probably arising out of feelings of guilt or uncleanness about sex. In Freudian terms, the white snake depicts the penis, the monster is sexual drive and the gun is again the penis, but in an aggressive mode. The dreamer, July, feels afraid of sex and is running away from facing this problem. But she cannot escape from her body and its needs.

> I have recurring dreams in which I am being chased or pursued. It is either a large white snake, a monster or a man with a gun chasing me — July.

In her book *Sexual Dreams*, Gayle Delaney quotes a dream which is problem-solving rather than problem-revealing.[55] The dreamer, Ilena, had strong repulsion against putting her boy friend's penis in her mouth, something he would like her to do. With Delaney's guidance, Ilena used the dream incubation technique (refer to Chapter Four) to see if she could find some insight into her feelings. She dreamt that 'she was naked with a man in a beautiful satin-and-lace bedroom. He lay on his back and asked, "Would you do this for me?"' Ilena knew he meant taking his penis into her mouth. As she looked at him, she realised deep inside that her dream lover would still love her deeply, even if she refused. This wiped away her feeling of repulsion and she wanted to give her lover pleasure. Ilena slowly licked every curve of his penis as if it were a sweet. Then she took his penis in her mouth and was thrilled at his sighs of delight.

This dream gave Ilena a completely new experience of making love. She saw clearly that the feeling of losing affection if she did not comply was behind her repulsion. Once Ilena realised she would be loved even if she refused, she was able in real life as well as in the dream to find a whole new sexual experience.

When considering your dreams, do not throw Freud out of the window. Guns, knives, bottles, a drum, piano or car can all suggest sexual feelings or urges. By being ready to admit your sexual feelings, they will step out from behind such symbols into the sort of direct sexual dream shown by Pete and Ilena.

If, like July, you are still running away from the snake, monster or shadowy man, use the technique of carrying the dream forward. Imagine yourself in the dream and turn to face what you have run from. Complete your love-making when it is frustrated in the dream by your fears. While awake, explore the dream to discover what other possibilities might be open to you. Be bold in your dreams and imagination. They are two totally safe areas in which you cannot get hurt. But you can learn a tremendous amount that will change the way you live in waking life.

Murder

Dreams are very literal. They portray in a seemingly real life event what we may be doing in a mental or emotional way. If someone is tortured by having their body injured, we can all see it and respond.

But if someone is tortured emotionally or mentally the wounds might not show. However, in our dreams the abstract is made real. When we are wounded, we dream of having a knife thrust in us. If sickened by what someone said or did to us we dream of vomiting. When we kill our love or creativity we dream of murder. The following example is typical:

> I dreamt my wife — a dream wife — had left me. In the middle of the night she came back to the house. I was so angry I murdered her. Because the children were with her and witnessed the murder, I killed them also and buried them under the floor of the house — Sean.

Sean had this dream — and others like it — when his wife, Jennie, began the menopause. Jennie withdrew from any sexual or emotional contact with him to such an extent he felt he was living in the house with a lodger rather than his wife. But Sean had not admitted to himself the extent of his feelings. This is why the bodies were buried — out of awareness. The children represented all the areas of growth and diversity present in the relationship that Sean had slain. In fact, he decided not to reach out to his wife while she consistently remained withdrawn from him. Sean had not killed his wife or children, but murdered his feelings for Jennie.

The murder is not just of love and contact. It can also be murdering yourself. This includes killing your sexual feelings, self-respect or creativity. In many cases it may not be that you kill yourself, but that something in you is killed by your relationship with a parent or loved one.

You must not forget that sometimes the murder is about real feelings for an exterior person, such as a brother, sister or spouse. If you cannot admit to such feelings and thereby transform them, they may be pressed into the unconscious until they break out in a far more destructive way. This sort of murder might be quite subtle. Instead of directly killing a parent or sibling, you could dream of going to their funeral and crying buckets, or see them sink beneath the waves in a tragic accident. This is not to say that all such dreams are a way of getting rid of difficult feelings you have about parents, siblings or partner. But you are the author/director of your dream dramas: nobody else pulled the trigger, arranged the funeral or sank the boat.[56]

In trying to understand such dreams, you must remember that it is necessary at some stage of your move to independence to 'kill' the enormous influence a parent has upon you. Many teenagers dream of killing a parent or seeing them die in some way. In such dreams you may feel enormous grief. After all, your parents have been an enormously important part of your early life. Also, it is difficult to become truly independent, so some of your fears are about the stress of what you face alone. Many of us escape this stress by transferring dependence from parents to a partner or organisation.

To get the best from such dreams, it is helpful to see them as a part of your change in growth. Perhaps what you have killed should be left to live. Through the miracle of dreams you can, with sympathy and understanding why and how you killed a part of yourself, allow a rebirth. But some factors do need to be killed and left behind, as heart-breaking as this may be. Only by exploring the dream and arriving at insight can such a decision about life or death be made.

Transformation
Dreams hang between the most primal in you and the most rational. They are children of the unconscious and self-awareness. They hold in them the jungle, raw nature, unexpurgated, primitive drives and longings as well as the highest of spiritual states. For the creator of dreams there is no fear of death or sex, or the bloody and slimy rivers of life coursing your body. Unlike your ego, this creator does not fear violence or religion. It stands master of all human experience, repulsed by nothing. If you are to learn from it, you need in some degree to be ready to encounter facets of experience for which you might usually have no sympathy. Only in this way do you become more than you were.

As a spark of awareness, you have travelled from conception to where you stand today. In terms of experience, rather than clock time you have spent an eternity in a pre-verbal condition. An aeon was lived before that in the womb. The enormous changes and adaptation needed to emerge from the womb and to wake to self-consciousness through the programming of language are perhaps forgotten in the eternal mists from which you arose. Even so, they left marks. Perhaps there were aspects of the change you did not manage fully, so no matter what physical age you are at present, you may still be very young emotionally or in terms of relationship.

Perhaps infantile jealousy, arising out of the savage urge to bond completely and possessively with your mother, still haunts you. Maybe you have not learned to love someone of the opposite sex, or claimed your gender self from the clutches of the parental images and influences held within you. It could be that you are still locked in the conflict between your own identity and society, feeling the need to fight and reject the Establishment. The conflict might be with your inner needs, showing itself as a battle with your appetite for food or sex, even air itself. The war with instincts can be as vicious as the battle with society, but in either case you are the casualty because you have missed your own wholeness. So death comes to some of us and we have never grown up, experienced love or moved beyond conflict.

It is the most moving tragedy, more than any film or book, to become aware that you have murdered your own beauty of sexuality or spirituality. To wake up in mid-life to the fact that you have never loved can be a rending experience. To see how your enormous energy has been spent in conflict is shattering. What a gift it is that within each of us is a power of transformation. Whatever we may think of the image of Christ Star Daily saw in religious terms, in dream terms it was a meeting with a transformative power. Star reached a point of transfor-

> ### STAR DAILY
>
> 'The plot to cause a mob riot was discovered and I was sentenced to the solitary. The average time for a strong man in solitary is fifteen days. This time came and went. I collapsed. Yet as I lay near death in the cell, a strange new thought came. I realised that I had been a dynamo of energy in everything I had done. What would have happened if I had used my powers for something other than destruction?
>
> 'As I lay near death, I dreamt of Jesus Christ, the man I had tried to avoid for many years. He seemed to stand near me. He looked down, deep into my eyes as though he was trying to penetrate my soul. In all my life I had never seen or felt such love.
>
> 'Before that experience, I was a callous criminal. After it, I was completely healed of my criminal tendencies! As a result, the prison doors swung open five years in advance of the time set for my release' — Star Daily. [57]

mation and went forward to a new life. Jung writes that 'Everyone must posses that higher level (of possible growth), at least in embryonic form, and in favourable circumstances, must be able to develop the possibility. When I examined the way of development of those persons who, quietly, and as if unconsciously, grew beyond themselves, I saw that their fates had something in common. Whether arising from without or within, the new thing came to all those persons from a dark field of possibilities; they accepted it and developed further by means of it . . .'[58]

The transcendent in us stands beyond particular forms or beliefs. It can appear in the person of a Christ or a Krishna, or as a sort of void. As the first it can bathe us in love, but in the second guise may frighten us. Caldwell describes a person meeting this second form as '. . . an astronaut sailing in a black void where directions have lost all meaning; up and down are useless terms, the polarities of life have ceased to exist. Nothing is true, everything is relative — not only time and space and direction but thoughts as well. He questions that the sky is blue . . . Nothing here but a shattered vision, broken into a thousand forms, qualities, movements, forces, ideas and feelings.'[59]

The strange aspect is that although this meeting threatens to take everything away that we hold dear, in fact it is healing. It lifts us beyond boundaries. It gives a new vision, liberation from all that held us captive. We emerge with a knowledge of the eternal. The meeting with the paradoxical nothingness breaks old attitudes, shattering the images we fashioned in the shape of gods, creeds and political beliefs. Seeing the shards and pieces, we realise they were made from our own ideas, hopes and fears. They were not the grand answers and divinities we had thought.

This does not take away the hard work of dealing with the great task of recognising and emerging from the massive programming received from the language we learnt, our parents and the culture in which we matured. These factors are like powerful, independent forces in us, shaping our actions, influencing decisions and often giving us hell. As a human animal — a mammal — we take from our parents a huge amount of ready-made responses to our environment.

What might eventually be seen as personal anxiety, a tendency to violence when confronted, an inability to deal with authority or any other personal idiosyncrasies are often received as patterns of behaviour that may reach back generations. Reptilian behaviour is imprinted as instinct. Mammals are different. They have a huge amount passed on by absorption from the parents. Unfortunately, what is transferred is not a refined and evaluated series of responses. We take on whatever our parents carried. The fact they survived, even if an alcoholic or violent, anti-social criminal, is enough to warrant the passage of their tendencies.

Most of us are lucky enough to be raised by reasonable parents and teachers. But we still need to incorporate and transcend the parental images and influences passed to us if we are to become a real person and not simply a replica of our parents and culture. Without this, we might constantly seek unsatisfying partners in love, or perhaps we do not know how to love as the response may not have been passed on. Caldwell, writing about the change that follows transformation of our images and programming, states that 'Once this is accomplished, they seek a love partner who correlates not to the mother, but to their own female selves. Successful female patients seek a correlation with their newly-freed male selves, and for both male and female, there comes a sense of healthy sexual completeness and balance.'

Such completeness does not arise from an occasional interest in what your dreams might reveal. It is only a prize for the dedicated and courageous explorer who undertakes a transformation of his life, perhaps because there seems no alternative but to change. But possibly such a player sees his life being like an artistic creation, needing as much frequent creative endeavour as the greatest of external undertakings.

In all of this, touching the inner power of transformation, the love, the void, that robs us of chains and imprisoning concepts, is vital. Wherever your dreams reveal it, grasp it and build it into your life. If it appears as a holy person, meditate on it and let its love or presence pervade you. If you meet it as a realisation, write that knowledge, paint it, act it out, live it. However it comes, it is the most precious of prizes.

7
Dreams: The Final Frontier

There is no final statement dreams make about life, death and the hereafter. But dreams — and thereby the unconscious — do seem to have a fairly consistent view of these big questions. This can be seen in the similarities between the multitude of myths and legends different cultures have created. Although details differ, the statement in such legends — themselves products of dreams and the unconscious — is that humans have a connection with the creative process of the universe. There is a frequently stated belief that your present life is not the only one, or that its end is not the termination of existence. Alongside this is the idea that 'As you sow, so shall you reap'. In other words, present events are not unconnected with what happened or was done in the past.

In the following pages I will try to summarise some of the viewpoints about life that emerge from people's insights as they explore their dreams. What is written will not be presented in a form of argument for these ideas. I will not try to justify them or seek evidence. I do not think this can be done with our present stage of scientific discovery. For instance, many verifiable psychic events, such as successful prediction, do not often arise in laboratory conditions. One of the possible reasons is that such phenomena are not based upon determination, but of a particular configuration of people, their attitudes, needs and longings. In other words, I might get an excellent result with a person who is deeply distressed and needs help, but no response at all when asked by a laboratory assistant to give a demonstration. Powerful life processes might function because of need, crisis, love and connectivity rather than critical reasoning.

What dreams have to say about life arises, I am sure, from such deeply felt processes within each of us.

Birth

Before the birth of my third son, I had a series of unusual dreams. In the first, I stood with my wife in a room. Both of us were afraid as the presence of an invisible being pervaded it. Then a voice spoke to assure us, saying: 'Do not be afraid. I have come to ask you to make love to form a body for me.'

The dream deeply impressed me. After hesitation and concerns about years of responsibility, my wife and I went ahead. Before we knew if conception had taken place — this was before the days of easy pregnancy testing — I had a dream in which I heard my wife sobbing. I went to find her, discovering she was pregnant, but it was a difficult pregnancy to bear. In a third dream we both knew it was a son she was carrying.

Such dreams are not unusual. A high proportion of women dream what gender and what temperament of child they are carrying. Of course, many 'pregnancy' dreams are about anxieties and other more psychological situations. But dreams such as these present the idea of a pre-existent being waiting for an appropriate birth situation and body in which to become involved; or the unborn personality directly asks to come into your life through being born to you. Some women told me they had such a strong experience of meeting their unborn while pregnant they had already bonded with their baby, and knew its temperament before birth occurred.

Robert van de Castle made a study of the dreams of pregnant women and found in many that the mother-to-be 'saw' what was happening inside her body. These dreams enabled the woman to see how her baby was developing, or if there were complications. Studies made by Carolyn Winget and Frederic Kapp suggested that many dreams about the growing baby were anxiety-based, and usefully released fears, making birth easier.

Dreams in adulthood that in exploration lead back to birth show that we can remember the deeply-engraved feelings experienced before and during our birth. Sometimes the theme of birth is presented in the form of meeting a person who was born with some difficulty, or the dream in some way has the theme of birth.

Although the view of birth that dreams offer overall is that the current personality draws its existence out of the past and does not come into the world new, it does not necessarily present the concept of reincarnation of a previous personality. The being from which you are born is timeless and has existed in all ages. Remembering the analogy of the hologram, the whole is in each part. Although you are in essence all things, because of the circumstances of your birth, body, gender, etc, you express and discover yourself as a unique personality, yet one connected with aspects of the past. The experience of colour can be used. On a sunny day at the beach people may have an enormous variety of coloured clothing. The one light touches them all. The texture and composition of the clothing they wear is what brings out a particular colour from the totality of light.

Drawn from this 'colourless' or timeless self is a particular theme or facet around which the present personality evolves. It is confronted by particular life experiences consistent with the theme being worked upon. Perhaps it is one of persecution or there is some work desired to be done. If so, the present personality is confronted by experiences of that nature. However, if it touches its own transcendent awareness, the difficulties or theme of its contemporary existence are seen as something only relevant to life in the current physical body. Nevertheless, at times a past personality does appear to return intact, as the following example suggests.

> An Italian couple, Captain and Mrs Battista, had a daughter who was born in Rome. The child was named Blanche. The couple employed a French-speaking Swiss 'Nanny' called Marie, who taught Blanche to sing a lullaby in French. Blanche loved the song and sang it repeatedly. Unfortunately, Blanche died, so Marie returned to Switzerland. Captain Battista writes: 'The cradle song, which would have recalled to us only too painful memories of our deceased child, ceased absolutely to be heard in the house . . . all recollection of it completely escaped our minds.
>
> Three years later Signora Battista became pregnant again. During the fourth month of her pregnancy she had a waking dream. Blanche appeared to her and said clearly, 'Mother, I am coming back!' When the child was born, it was once more a girl. Because of Signora Battista's insistence she was named Blanche.

Nine years after the death of the first Blanche, when the second Blanche was six years of age, an extraordinary phenomenon happened. To quote Captain Battista:

While I was with my wife in my study which adjoins our bedroom, we heard, both of us, like a distant echo, the famous cradle song. The voice came from the bedroom, where we had put our little daughter Blanche fast asleep . . . We found the child sitting up on the bed and singing with an excellent French accent the cradle song, which neither of us had certainly ever taught her. My wife asked her what it was she was singing. The child, with the utmost promptitude, answered that she was singing a French song. 'Who taught you this pretty song?' I asked her. 'Nobody. I know it out of my own head', she replied. [60, 61]

Death

In his book *Death Dreams*, Kenneth Paul Kramer says that 'Our investigation begins with the unconscious because that is the domain in which unadulterated (or as close as possible) expressions of the death-instinct can be seen to interact with awareness.'[62]

Most of us dream of death frequently. If we examine such dreams, we come face-to-face with the figure of death many times. In doing so, we work out a relationship not so much with the fact of death, but concepts — and particularly our feelings — about it. If we persist, the dreams that arise and the experiences we have in exploring such events can be deeply moving and beautiful. From them arise our personal philosophy and strength to meet life and death.

In being told thousands of dreams, I have seen that the death of someone close to us often presents itself in a dream. A friend's son woke one morning troubled and told his mother that he was very distressed by a dream about a school friend. In the dream, he was with his friend near a door. His acquaintance, a young man, opened the door, beyond which was a beautiful landscape, and went through. When the dreamer tried to follow him, he was stopped and could not pass through the door. On arriving at school that day, he discovered that his friend had died in a motor-bike accident on the way to school.

Another person told me that in a dream he was walking with a long-standing friend. They came to a river. The friend crossed the river, but the dreamer could not and woke very disturbed. He found later that the friend who appeared in the dream had died about the time he dreamt of the river crossing.

Dreams often portray death as a change, as in these examples. Passing through the door or crossing a river depict a shifting from one place or condition to another. They do not in any way show an ending of the personality, but illustrate how the person who is still alive in the body cannot share the change.

The many dreams of those who have undergone a near-death experience portray death as a time of meeting and digesting your life. All that you have done is placed against a more inclusive or universal life. These experiences suggest that your personal life is measured against the collective spirit of humankind. It is also quite clearly portrayed that in losing your body you enter into a world akin to dreams.

It is a world or condition in which your very thoughts, attitudes and emotional tone become real as an exterior environment. In this condition, thoughts and emotions are creative forces to an unimaginable extent. So what sort of world would a person filled with anger or darkness create for himself? What kind of world would an individual who was bubbly and loving create? Here is certainly where the concepts of heaven and hell as distinct places arose.

Taken as a whole, the death state is not shown in dreams as something of which to be afraid. It is more like an awakening after a long, troubling sleep. Sometimes, it is depicted as returning home after being held in a foreign country, as in the following example:

> I dreamt I was dying or dead. It felt like my own little life had merged into everything and become a part of it. This was blissful, like being at peace and still. In trying to describe this, I have to use the image of a great mural painted on a cliff face. The mural has trees and grass, animals and humans. I am one of the humans in the picture and have stepped out of the mural to become three-dimensional. Being three-dimensional is everyday life. This is life as an individual with all its difficulties.

But at death, I step back into the mural again. I fade into the background of life again and disappear. This is wonderful. My sense of self recedes and there is a blissful merging with all things. I want to stay there forever, to go to sleep into this ocean of blissfulness. I feel that I could stay there for a hundred years, and if I then took a breath I would emerge from the mural again and take up my everyday life just as I left it off, except that events will have moved on. I want to do this — Tom.

The face of death is therefore not an unpleasant one when we have looked beyond our fears conjured-up by the awful images our culture erects. As Tom suggests, meeting death is meeting all of life. It is a time to harvest, to digest all we have gathered. This beautiful description portrays something of this:

For me it was a total re-living of every thought I had ever thought, every word I had ever spoken, and every deed I had ever done; plus the effect of each thought, word and deed on everyone and anyone who had ever come within my environment or sphere of influence, whether I knew them or not (including unknown passers-by on the street) — P. H. Atwater.[63]

This last piece attempts to convey the final meeting with everything and everyone when death stands revealed:

All of a sudden, I see the face of Death. I hear its voice. I know it, for we have met often and always. Death has the features of a child I made cry; the profile of my loved woman; your countenance. Have I known you? Then I have known Death. Have I betrayed any? Then I have betrayed Death. And death's face is beauty for it is all things — naked, undressed of flesh, leafless, exposed, unclad Life — without the garment which our selfhood is — Mathew H.

Destiny

At birth you enter a very particular and unique set of circumstances. The genes you inherit carry certain tendencies of strength or weakness. You may inherit a certain physical strength or weakness. Your parents, time of birth in the history of events and the culture into which you are born — along with social status, financial wealth, education and parents' background — are all deeply influential factors.

The effect of these factors upon shaping your personality and response to them creates what can be thought of as a personal destiny. In other words, you have a tendency towards certain interests and actions or ways of acting. But the word 'destiny' is often defined as 'an unalterable fate' whereas dreams depict it more as a destination towards which we move. Perhaps this is like a compass always swinging to point in a certain direction, no matter how it is swung about.

This links with what was said about birth and the bringing into incarnation of a certain theme — or themes — to deal with and transcend. But the more one considers the wisdom of dreams, the more it seems that there may be several threads to the possibility of destiny. This is what one dream explorer says about her intuitions when exploring a dream:

Suddenly, towards the end of working on my dream, I seemed to leap beyond anything I had ever experienced before. Instead of being someone separated from everybody else living a certain day in time, I was a river that flowed through all time. I had always existed and was involved in all history.

As this happened, I knew just as clearly as in ordinary life I know my name that a life had been lived in which the 'I' of that person had been persecuted for their religious beliefs. In persecution, some of their family had been killed, and as that person I had made a decision never again to trust people. The decision brought about the desire to live isolated from human group activity.

With an amazing heightened vision, I could see this influence flowing through all my present life, subtly shaping it. The things I had chosen to do or work at were all connected, either as a means of trying to change that decision or as an expression of it — Tracy M.

Tracy tells us that her 'destiny' arose out of a long past. But it is equally true that your destiny arises from passions and pains etched into you from your present history. You may fight for those who are oppressed because you have been oppressed. You might search for meaning because you were fed lies. The passions that move you are often overlooked in the duties of daily life. Dreams remind you from where your greatest energy and creativity arise.

Dr Melvin Morse, a Washington-based paediatrician, studied critically ill children at the University of Washington School of Medicine, recording their experiences as they were dying or resuscitated. He quotes the words of one child who was resuscitated, and says they are typical of what children experience/dream as they near death:

> Gosh, something really weird happened to me, and if you promise not to laugh, I'll tell you. I thought I was floating out of my body, and I saw a light, and there were a lot of good things in that light. One boy said that he was told, 'You can come back later, but you have a job to do now'.[64]

As they brush with death, adults also have this message of a job to undertake. The task is not usually anything fancy. It is to live one's life and harvest its experience. In this way we are all gardeners in the vineyard.

When you read through your dreams kept over a long period of time, another strange view of destiny can arise. You read again and again scenes and ideas that in years after the dream was recorded become material facts of your life. Are your dreams predicting your future? If so, perhaps what you do is pre-destined. But another explanation is nearer to what happens. In dreams, do you express your hidden desires and urgent drives? If so, to a large extent it appears you create the future from your thoughts and fantasies, your pains and longings. All of the past is with you now as influences and responses. The future is here in the present as possibilities. You are a rolling ball, carrying all past, present and future.

Illness and Misfortune

The unconscious is like an immense storage box that has everything in it. Not only are there wonderfully effective medicines and healing information, but toys, tricks, pieces of behaviour no longer used, memorabilia and items other people have left. Sometimes we discover in this box promissory notes that seem very difficult to claim. I mean that we may find in our dreams and unconscious statements that we can be perfectly healthy and happy, very wealthy and with wonderful talents.

Claiming these promises may be altogether harder than receiving them. Nevertheless, in many years of travelling the unconscious, I do not see it producing lies. What may happen is that we place our own interpretation or hopes on what is experienced. Our dream could be a reflection of our own deep desire that a particular event may happen rather than a prediction that it will.

Transformation of health and of one's inner feelings of pain or despair can happen. The power of life within us is always there to be tapped. It is like a fountain in which we can bathe, finding healing and peace. However, there is a strange paradox in it. Ronnie Laing, writing in his poem *Bird Of Paradise*[65] says, 'The truth I am trying to grasp is the grasp that is trying to grasp it.' Later he adds: 'The Life I am trying to grasp is the me that is trying to grasp it. There is really nothing more to say when we come back to that beginning of all beginnings that is nothing at all. Only when you begin to lose that Alpha and Omega do you want to start to talk and to write, and then there is no end to it, words, words, words.'

As Laing suggests, part of the paradox is that what we want, we have to be. To get well, you have to be well. But how can you be well when you are sick? Your dreams will help in this by putting you in touch with powerful images from, or through which, the energy of your wholeness can flow into dis-ease. Sometimes the healing symbol may be in the form of a wonderful circle, a mandala. It might be like a beautiful jewel, a healing fountain or a radiant, love-emanating person. Here is an example. Even though this is not your dream, it is nevertheless a healing symbol that you can use by opening to its centre.

> In the dream, I looked over at a plain wall in the room. It was light green. To my amazement a huge living and wondrous circle appeared on the wall. It was full of movement, everything dancing in time to music. At the very centre of the circle was emptiness, nothing, a void. Yet out of this nothingness all things emerged.
>
> There were plants, animals, people, hills, rivers and mountains, all coming to birth. They danced out in their own individual movement, yet each unknowing was part of the whole wonderful and intricate dance, which made a great pattern and movement in the body of the circle. All

danced to the periphery and there turned and moved, still in their ballet, back to the centre. At that centre, they plunged into its oblivion again. But at that very moment new life sprang from it to dance once more — Bonnie.

To touch that centre and be renewed by it, you may have to surrender to it, to let things happen. You need to hold it as an image and drop into the centre with as much trust as you can. By doing so you are opening to the primal essence in you for renewal, for guidance — a guide in the dance. You may be out of step, even with yourself. That is your sickness.

Alongside the surrender, however, you may also need a focused and penetrating intelligence. Few of us are healed miraculously with only faith as our key. The rest may have to dig into the unconscious through dreams to find the steps to help us retrace our way to that centre. These steps are usually made up of events in your life that have led you to make certain decisions, to take particular directions, to hold specific grudges and pains. In undoing these, you also undo your sickness. Even if the knives you find embedded in your heart were pressed there by those you loved, discovering them leads to strength. The burdens you carry have shaped your power and sensitivity.

Marriage and Relationships

Gaining information from dreams is one of the most powerful aids to understanding and improving your relationships. But this chapter is about what dreams have to say about relationships, not how to improve them.

The philosophy of the unconscious as it shows itself through dreams is that in our essence we are neither male nor female, but a being transcending such polarities. We are also an integral part of a great ocean of life. There is only separation when you view the world through your physical senses and the concept of your identity, as in the following dream:

A small speed boat was at sea. But the sea dissolved anybody who fell in. One man did so, but held himself together as a blob of water and jumped back to the speedboat. I remember the words, 'The sea is a great solvent' — Anthony.

In Anthony's dream, the man and the sea are one and the same. He can come out of it and be an individual, or plunge into it and merge as one with it. This is important when you consider relationships and whether there is such a thing as a soul mate or perfect partner. Does the drop merged in the ocean relate more to one drop than to another? The droplet living as a 'blob of water' in time and space certainly relates more fully to some people than to others, simply from being in closer proximity in one way or another.

One of the great principles the unconscious frequently presents in dreams is that we create each other — that we are made up of countless other people. Even your mind is not your own. You have individual thoughts, but your means of thinking them is ancient and not your own. Language preceded you and will survive your individual life. You were immersed in it at birth and gradually learned it. You certainly never initiated even a few of the words you use or the concepts you hold. So from where did they originate?

Even the energy in your body, the oxygen you breathe and the minerals of your bones have been recycled, perhaps many times. The sun gave you energy. It was taken up by plants, and then absorbed into your body and used. Similarly, your ideas and attitudes have almost entirely been passed to you from others. Who was the first human to punch another in the face? And who was the first to share a portion of food with another? Observation of a monkey group has shown that the innovation of washing sand out of rice practised by one female monkey was taken up by the whole group and became an accepted practice for further generations.

According to the unconscious, love is a sort of eating each other, a taking of someone else into yourself.[66] This love can become so deep that in some way you blend with each other in some degree just as Anthony's man merged with the sea. At such a time you learn, or take into yourself, an enormous amount from the loved one. What appears to be telepathy emerges as you know each other so deeply, sharing thoughts and feelings at the same moment. If a loved one dies, there is no real separation because you hold them inside you so fully. The pain is from their physical absence, but much of this may be out of dependence rather than love.

With children, if you dare to be parents instead of baby-sitters, the unconscious shows again and again in dreams that from giving yourself to another you receive an immense spiritual reward. This is not something you can gain from the exterior world. Giving of yourself is a fundamental part of nature. The sun pours out energy to you. The earth offers itself as food for living creatures in combination with the sun's energy. The 'Big Bang' was perhaps a huge act of self-giving through death so that otherness could exist. In giving, you develop a link of sympathy with the heart of life itself. If you have learnt that self-giving, you find that the doors to the temple of life in the unconscious are open to you. If you have fought for your children through love, you are kin with the millions of other life forms, whether tigress or sparrow, who give themselves so fully to their offspring. Life knows you and welcomes you to its heart and secrets.

> My emotions were ripped open as if I were being burst or torn apart in my soul. I managed to gasp out between cries that I had been in this place so many times — the Temple of the Animals — but always in the past with a closed heart. I realised as I was opened more and more that it was not my heart that was closed. It was that I had always been too proud. I had been shutting out the common animal. I had killed my sexuality, my common humanity, because I wanted to be different. I did not want to be like the common herd who had, I felt, rejected me. I wished to be above them. But now I felt the most extraordinary love and wisdom as I stood before all the animals — Sandra.

Relationship is at the heart of information we gather from the unconscious. Love is the key to relationship, but not what society usually calls love. That is a sort of dependent, romantic, perhaps child-like, form of love. The love presented by the unconscious is about the ability to take another being into yourself. It is the strength to give of your being to another as an animal does when we eat it or the sperm enters the ovum and the two different worlds totally die to each other to create new life. The world works out of this sort of relationship. And through this type of relationship you can slowly become more than you were. You gradually gain strength to allow more of life to be felt and known. In the end this widening sympathy is what leads to an experience of the transcendent.

Sex

Writing about her experience of frigidity and how she found release, Constance Newland says: 'I would like to emphasise that I achieved this cure for myself. I believe one can achieve psychic health without recourse to therapy. It is only when one fights a consistently losing battle against an important problem one needs help.'[67]

The full flowering of the sexual feelings is a subject of many dreams, as with the following:

> I looked in the mirror and saw that my face had certain 'Mongol' features, especially the lower lip. I realised I had always had these, but they had remained latent. In the dream, I knew that this was Bright's disease, of which I would surely die. Then it came to me that this had all come about through not having sex, and if I started again the features would go — Rosie.

It does not seem to be important in dreams that you have genital sex. What is vital is that you engage in sexual intercourse. The difference is that with genital sex there may be very little 'intercourse' or relationship between yourself and your partner. According to dreams, it is the relationship and blending of different personalities that are the vital centre of sex. The sex drive pushes you towards personal transcendence, if only momentarily. The most awful sex confronts you with another person, even if you are brutal in that meeting. I am not suggesting such brutality is acceptable, only that the drive makes you confront someone other than yourself. Without it you might never attempt anything other than a superficial relationship. Through sex there is the possibility that you may take in another person's being and become more.

Sex is the most powerful form of transcendence we have. It transcends religion, politics, physical difference, skin colour, age and culture. You and I extend beyond the narrow boundary of ourselves and dare to want another person, to need, to admit we are not self-contained. Clumsy as it may be, lovers want, offer, take and give. Without love, there would only be containment, isolating and isolated. There would be no need to take-in what a lover offers; there would be no absorbing and growing from the infinite richness of another being's difference.

The Final Frontier

In her book *Dream Power*, Ann Faraday writes that from her research stretching over twenty years, she sees that the vast majority of a person's dreams are about a 'reflection of our everyday lives and conflicts'. She adds that as we use such dreams to get more in 'touch with ourselves and with the myriad processes that are taking place all the time just below the surface of conscious awareness' so our growth will 'open up other, more mysterious aspects of dream life...'[68]

Some of these 'other' and mysterious aspects of dreams have already been mentioned, but it is worth defining certain of the possibilities more fully. They illustrate the immense possibilities of human potential.

Although Charles Tart has written extensively about this, some of the most fascinating research was done by Stanislav Grof while observing clients undertaking drug-assisted psychotherapy. Along with Jung, Grof noticed that exploring the unconscious in a consistent way not only enabled an individual to overcome personal conflicts and problems, but also revealed a continuity of communication between the conscious and unconscious. It appeared there was a drive from the unconscious to clear unfinished business and conflicts in order to move into areas uncharted by Western psychology.

When his clients started experiencing events such as memories of life in the womb, Grof thought they were pure fantasy. But he checked whatever information was given and found to his astonishment that the memories often connected with real events or environments.[69] Prior to this finding, Grof had been a conventional psychiatrist working within the limited attitudes of his training. As he checked patients' experiences, his direction changed, although at first he was not inclined to share his findings with professional colleagues. It is difficult to summarise Grof's discoveries because they are so extensive, but here is a short list:

● *Memory of Uterine Life* — People who gained these memories were convinced that as a foetus they subjectively experienced all their mother felt. This included attempted abortion, sounds, the mother's distress if she were ill, her emotions of pleasure, anger or hate and sexual arousal as well as being unwanted or loved. They could feel the effect of alcohol, nicotine or other drugs. For some there was the memory of uterine bliss and union with the mother.

- *Experiencing Ancestors* — Grof said that in certain people the experience was of ancestors fairly near in time, such as grandparents or great-grandparents. But sometimes they felt as if they broke out of their usual limits of memory and found deep knowledge of ancient ancestors. These regressions were felt to be very much a part of the sub-strata of the person's present life. I have experienced this. What I met gave me an enormously enlarged understanding of my grandfather, my father and my own life tendencies. My recovery of 'memory' was of several hundred years in the past. It arose from exploring what appeared to be a simple dream.[70] My sense was that I was not reading my genetic code, but a heritage of behaviour strategies passed to me unconsciously by my father.

- *The Racial or Collective Unconscious* — This differs from meeting one's ancestors in that it does not bring definite information about how your present personality has grown out of ancestral or parental experience. What you meet is an experience of cultures and historical periods not directly related to you. It is nevertheless an amazing experience, bringing a rich understanding of the lives and destiny of a race, and its gift to the present. Grof reports an example where the person experienced himself as an embalmer in ancient Egypt. From it, he was able to 'describe the size and quality of the mummy bandages, materials used in fixing the mummy cloth, and the shape and symbolism of the four canopic[71] jars and the corresponding canopic chests'.

- *Evolutionary Forms* — Knowing oneself as an ancient animal or experiencing the summarised sense of evolution through millions of years. Many people have met this. It feels as if all evolution is summarised in your own body. Giving awareness to your cells allows their experience to be acted out, like playing a tape. A tape is only composed of electromagnetic traces, but we experience these as sound or video by using a machine.

- *Past Incarnations* — The memory of a past life linked with the present is quite common. This has already been mentioned elsewhere (see the sections on Birth and Destiny). All that needs to be added here is that Grof reports that these memories have the theme of revealing important loves, hates or work that have carried over from the past and need to be worked out or extended in the present life. They expose the apparent injustices of the present in disabilities or impoverishment as having their roots in the past. Grof's comment on this is:

> The opening of the area of past-incarnation experiences . . . is sometimes preceded . . . by instructions received intuitively that introduce the individual to the fact of reincarnation, make him recognise the responsibility for his past deeds, and present the law of karma[72] as an important part of the cosmic order that is mandatory for all sentient beings.

● Because there is not space to consider all the many aspects Grof saw in his thousands of clients, I will list some without comment — Meetings with the dead — Encountering non-human intelligences or god-like beings — Being at-one with all life — Experiencing creation — Other universes — Intuitive understanding of cultural or religious symbols — Identification with plants and minerals — Extraordinary healing of sickness — Time travel.

So far we have not found a boundary to what is possible in certain states of consciousness. Because these various possibilities have not been well explored, we do not yet know, for instance, what it really means to feel you have travelled in time. What do you find if you touch 'another universe', for example? Is it a purely subjective and personal experience relating to one's own growth? Or is it in some way an observation of an objective reality?

8
Dream Questions Answered

Why does my lover/partner reject me in my dreams?
Most dreams where someone important rejects you are dealing with your own fear of not being loveable, or concern at being deserted by the person to whom you are attached. The following is an example:

> Last night I dreamt my wife was trying to get me out of her life, and out of the house. It was as if she was attempting to push me into a feeling of tension and rejection which would make me leave — Gopi.

Gopi had been raised by his grandmother, who died when he was nearly two. This led to feelings of loss about the person he loved. However, sometimes such a dream may hide a secret wish to leave the partner. Their apparent rejection would give you an excuse to do so. This next dream is about a different situation:

> My husband is with me on holiday, but for the whole of the time I seldom see him. If I do see him, he is with other people, and completely ignores me. He only once spoke to me and said, 'You never, ever loved me!' I woke up sobbing. Why does he always reject me in my dreams? He died nearly seven years ago, after thirty-six years of marriage. We had no children; we lived only for each other — Mrs E. C.

E's husband has indeed 'left her' because of his death. Her dream dramatises this and goes on to show her feeling uncertain about the love that existed. This may be due to E taking the loss as a sign that she did not love him enough. Rejection should not be accepted in your dreams. Ask yourself where such feelings of rejection emanate. Understand the roots. Determine to get the love you want and need in your dreams, and in life. Put into words what the original message was from the one you trusted to love you — i.e. it might have been,

'I was not good enough to love.' Now change the message into something creative in the present — i.e. 'If I give love, I deserve love in return.'

Do the dead talk to us in our dreams?

This is a very difficult question to answer with certainty. We would need confirmation from the dead person that a message was given and clearly received. However, some dreams do have the appearance of specific communications.

> When I was engaged to be married, I agreed to meet my fiancé at an hotel one weekend. The night before I travelled to the hotel, my dead mother appeared to me in a dream. Curtains were pulled back. She walked out, looked at me tenderly and said, 'My darling, your marriage cannot be.' I felt frightened by this dream. The next day, while I waited for my fiancé at the hotel a message came. He had been killed in a car crash on his way to me. The dream helped me enormously to deal with his death — Mary.

Mary was assured by this dream that her mother's love was caring for her and watching over her. Although the dream brought bad news, it also convinced her of continuing life.

We often dream about people we know who are dead, but few of these dreams have the same power as Mary's experience. Also, they do not often give information about the dead person's present situation. Rather than a communication, perhaps they should be regarded as an insight or connection with the dead person.

Such dreams usually have quite specific themes. They contain some sort of representation of the person's death, or of their departure or separation from the dreamer and physical life. Lastly, they are about the state of — and onward journey — of the dead individual concerned. After the death of someone to whom we are attached, sometimes we have a long series of dreams in which we gradually let go of them. The following is typical of this sort of dream:

> Two years after my husband's death, I dreamt he came to me and said he would not be coming back. With that he vanished, leaving me with my hands to my face in shock. As he spoke to me, he had a concerned or even distressed look on his face. I asked him, 'But what about me?' to which he

replied: 'Don't worry. Everything will be all right for you.' It was after this remark he vanished. I was awakened by hearing myself say, 'I have got to let him go.' We had been married thirty-three years.

How can I help my child with his/her dreams and nightmares?
Dreams — and even nightmares — are psychologically healthy, and a means of releasing fears and tension. However, if children are haunted by nightmares and wake with great distress, they obviously need support and help. Most youngsters have nightmares at some time. Childhood is, after all, a vulnerable stage. We face many fears and uncertainties, with few adult skills or props to confront them. As children, we are not allowed alcohol and nicotine to use as socially acceptable drugs to suppress anxiety. The dream below shows how a child's concerns can centre around a parent:

> When I was about eight years old, I often used to have an abstract nightmare. It consisted of me (a soft, wavy line) being attacked by the enemy (a pointed, zigzag line). As the enemy (zigzag) overcame me (soft waves), I would wake up in terror. The nightmares ended when my father died unexpectedly from a heart attack.

The aim in helping with nightmares is to support the child to release and move beyond the fears. Often such nightmares have a wild animal or dark creature, or connect directly with a parent — i.e. losing them or feeling threatened. The animals represent the child's unsocialised fears and emotions. They chase the child because he or she feels pursued or cannot escape from them. The specific help we can give is to aid them in containing and finding a different relationship with their feelings. With the case expressed in the example, the child would obviously have had to play out his fear regarding his father. But in such an instance there might not have been any escape if the father had not died. Some well-meaning parents have no idea that they terrify their child. They fail to see the body language or facial expression of anxiety, showing their offspring's fear.

However, sketching or painting the dream can often help enormously. Get the child to draw the dream and talk over each part of the picture. If there are any frightening aspects, tell the youngster he or she can draw that part again and alter it — for instance, put the animal/creature in a cage. Caging the frightening part often produces immediate change. When the child feels more confident about the caged creature, he or she can start to make friends with it. Here the aim is to get the animal's power, its strength, or whatever magic abilities it possesses. This may take a series of drawings and talks.

Your child can also be helped by talking about positive dreams. These can be very supportive and encouraging. This is because they usually centre around issues that are extremely important at a feeling level. Talking about the dream is a safe way of dealing with such issues. One example is that children face the task of becoming independent in everyday ways, like preparing their breakfast or turning taps on and off to get a drink. This situation may be represented by a caged pet, who has to have everything done for it. Talking this over, with suggestions about where a start might be made towards independence, can be a great gift.

Does everybody dream?
Laboratory testing on a huge variety of people shows that all of us dream each night. Even individuals who claim they never sleep have been found to cat-nap during the night without awareness of having slept, and dream during these periods. The only exception was a man who had been injured in the head by shrapnel. It damaged the part of his brain that dealt with dreams.

The real question is why some of us do not remember our dreams. There are several possible reasons for this. One of the foremost is that we might have ignored them for so long we have the entrenched habit of pushing them aside as we wake. People who become interested in their dreams find they start to recall them easily. Tests have shown that interest and intention to remember are major factors in dream recall.

Another reason for forgetting is that we each have a threshold between waking and sleeping, perhaps like a swing door. In some people, it is very heavy and hard to swing. This 'heaviness' is possibly made up of physiological and psychological tendencies. It is known, for instance, that B vitamins help to strengthen this threshold, making it more difficult for fantasy material or feelings to stream into consciousness from the unconscious. This is sometimes used in aiding people to control difficult feelings. But some individuals have a body type that is already strong in this way while others find they possess a very volatile feeling range and easy access to fantasies or even hallucinations, which used to be called visions. The psychological factors are that many people completely discount imagination and feelings, suppressing them from conscious life.

How do drugs affect dreaming?
One of the most common social drugs of great power is alcohol. Many people use it as a suppressant in connection with anxiety or depression, and also to help them sleep. Although alcohol appears to work in these cases, its helpfulness is only very temporary, leading to further use and perhaps even habitual excess. The effect of alcohol is quickly to muffle anxiety or sleeplessness. But our body changes much of the alcohol into aldehydes, which create restlessness and fitful sleep. Alcohol also inhibits REM sleep.

Considering that laboratory tests on inhibiting REM sleep brought about increasing mental distress, this is an insidious effect, once more leading to the possible need to use more alcohol to suppress its own side-effects. Carlyle Smith, of Trent University in Peterborough, Ontario, has shown that for an average-sized person, the alcohol in just over two pints of beer knocks out about fifty per cent of the normal amount of REM sleep in the first half of the night.

A study carried out by Jean Knox and published in the Journal of Analytical Psychology[73] showed how heavy alcohol use impairs the capacity to digest new information and experience. This causes resistance to change, making it difficult to face loss, and depressive anxiety.

Studies performed at the Texas South-Western Medical Center, Department of Psychiatry, Sleep Study,[74] found that depressed patients using the anti-depressants fluoxetine and nefazodone showed extremely low dream recall. The content of dreams was also changed, making them less vivid and detailed. To quote, 'It is possible that the lack of change in the emotional tone of dreams in treatment responders[75] may reflect a continuing vulnerability to depression.'[76] Other studies using the drug trimipramine led to a positive influence on dream tone and recall.[77]

Investigating the recovery of alcoholics and the drug addicted through their dreams, Reed Morrison suggests there are five stages of recovery. He names these as Pandora's box, dragon fight, rebirth, descent, and return.[78]

What is the point of predictive dreams?
Louisa Rhine, wife of the famous ESP researcher Dr J. B. Rhine,[79] examined over twenty thousand cases of ESP and precognition. She placed her findings in categories of intuitions, dreams, hallucinations and PK[80] phenomena. Louisa's research showed that precognitions occurred more frequently than any other form of extended perception. Other studies found that about sixty to sixty-eight per cent of all precognitions occur during dreaming. Michael Talbot writes, 'We may have banished our ability to see the future from our conscious minds, but it is still very active in the deeper strata of our psyches.'[81]

Research done by Louisa and her husband and such people as Ullman and Krippner make it unnecessary to argue the case for dream ESP.[82] It is still a largely unexplored field, one not generally accepted in other branches of science. From the purely personal point of view, many people ask what purpose — if any — a precognitive dream has. The reason they do so is because having experienced such a dream and seeing the predicted event happen, they wonder what the point was in knowing. From their viewpoint, foreknowledge only added to the anxiety. This is often because the person involved, although feeling anxious about the dream, did nothing about it.

Such dreams are centres of great power. They not only demonstrate that we are in touch with the transcendent within us, but also offer the opportunity to change events. One concept of this is of a 'branching future'. This means our choice can alter the direction we are taking. The following cases illustrate this possibility.

The nineteenth-century suffragette Susan B. Anthony dreamt the hotel in which she was staying caught fire. She left it — and the hotel did indeed catch fire. More recently, a woman dreamt her twenty-month-old daughter was dangerously balanced on a window-ledge. The dream woke her and she ran to check on the baby's safety. All was well. But three weeks later, when the mother was outside hanging washing on a line she realised her daughter was still indoors. Rushing to the child's room, she found her daughter balanced on the window-sill and pulled her to safety.

In another case, a woman woke from a nightmare in which her son was caught in an hotel fire. The mother knew her son was away on business, but did not know where, so could not phone him. She therefore knelt in prayer, asking for his safety. At that time, the son dreamt he heard his mother calling him urgently. He woke to discover the hotel on fire and was able to get out safely.

Jaime Castell used that power of change when he experienced such a warning dream. In 1978, his wife had just become pregnant. Three months before the baby was born, Jaime dreamt a disembodied voice told him that he would die before the child arrived. Acting on the dream, he took out a hefty insurance, payable only at his death. Just a few weeks later while driving along a motorway, a car travelling at great speed in the opposite direction crashed out of control through the central barrier. It landed on top of Jaime's car, killing him instantly.

Other people who have had similar warning dreams may pray for help or visualise a different outcome. They have lived to experience a near miss, avoided because they remained aware of a critical point being reached.

Do dreams of death mean I am doing to die soon?
We all dream of dying, but few predict your death or that of another person. Most explore feelings about death, breaking through to a more creative relationship with it. Sometimes such 'practise' dreams are obvious. We face death and realise there are many things we still want to do before we go. The dream is thereby reminding us of the important issues in our life. If you have a series of dreams suggesting illness or death and they worry you, seek a medical examination. Your future is yours to make. The direction you take can be altered. Your changing attitudes and way of life reshape the future.

People *do* have warning dreams about the death of a relative, or even their own demise. These dreams usually carry a strong conviction of their message, and are not simply anxiety dreams.

How can I conquer my fears in dreams?
Working with anxiety dreams is one of the best ways of meeting fears. To do this, use the questions given in Chapter Four under

Processing Dreams. Especially adopt the technique described in which you carry your dreams forward to more satisfying conclusions.

Why do I keep having the same dream?
Recurring dreams occur due to several factors. They arise because of buried anxieties or you are returning to fundamental attitudes and life lessons. Regarding this last reason, the foundations for your character traits were laid down at certain times. For instance, the house in which you lived as a young child may be used in your dreams to represent the life lessons or attitudes you developed at the time. Your school might be utilised to depict the life lessons impressed on you during teen years. These original scenes appear again and again in your dreams as you are confronted by, or evolve, the attitudes and responses you developed in connection with those places.

If it is a nightmarish or anxiety dream, the recurrence usually happens because your unconscious is trying to heal fears or hurts you experienced and buried in past years. To heal such hurts, the unconscious tries to push them to the surface to make you aware of them. This is necessary because the repression of such strong feelings is rather like cutting off a hand and wrapping it in cling film because it hurt. If this happens several times we are left with much less energy and mental resources than we had when we were born. To reconnect with the part of you, with the buried energy and experience once more, means feeling the hurts you avoided in the past.

To do this, use the techniques outlined in Chapter Four under the heading of *Acting In*, and the sub-heading *And Then What?* This is where you continue the dream in imagination to some sort of satisfying conclusion. Also read the section in Chapter Six on recurring dreams.

What makes me move or fight in my sleep?
> I am twenty, married, and terrified of spiders. I dream I am in bed when a spider falls on me and crawls under the sheets. I see it clearly and leap screaming out of bed. My husband tries to calm me, but sometimes I punch him. I nearly broke his nose one night. I am only seven stone, but in my sleep I am a fighter. Can you help me? — Mary.

Mary is not alone in her enormous activity while dreaming or in seeing the spider while still awake. Pippa M describes her experiences as follows:

> The most alarming nightmares have been to do with spiders. I have felt them crawling over the bed-clothes, over me and the sheets, and under the bed covers to the extent where I have to get out of bed and brush them away. I can still see them after I have woken.

While dreaming, the brain sends messages to make our body move just as it does when we are awake and active. Usually part of the brain — the pons — inhibits these impulses, allowing us to remain quietly asleep. However, occasionally the excitement or fear we feel in a dream overrides the inhibition and we start to move or talk in our sleep. This may cause the most amusing or disturbing events to happen. If, as with Pippa and Mary, these dream movements and hallucinations occur often, they need to be treated in the same way as suggested under recurring dreams.

Can one really dream the same dream as someone else?

> Some years ago, I woke from a terrible dream in which I was backed against a wall and my elder sister was stabbing me with scissors. Later that day, at work my sister phoned me to say she'd had an awful dream last night in which she stabbed me. Can you explain this? — Brenda S.

Sharing a dream with the same details is uncommon, but does happen to some people. The next example illustrates how a link can be created by love, not sibling anger::

> My husband is in the Navy, serving on a ship in the Gulf. We have always been close, through twenty-two years. I dreamt we were making love, and could even smell him. It ended as love-making always does for us, with orgasm and a cuddle into deep sleep. I woke surprised he was not next to me. He phoned next day to say he had the same dream on the same night — Mrs E. H.

These shared dreams demonstrate the possibility of our awareness going beyond our own boundaries in dreams. Each of us enters this realm of the collective mind when we sleep, but few bring back such definite memories.

What can I do if I keep having nightmares?
Nightmares are often expressions of fears we have not faced or admitted to while awake. The dream will usually give a clue to what causes the fear. If the dream includes a child, for example, it may be a concern you developed in childhood. If it features an animal, it could be related to your powerful urges, such as sex or anger. If it shows darkness, the worry might be about what is unknown or imagined.

Initially, look at the nightmare in this way to define, if only vaguely, with what the fear might connect. Then imagine yourself in the action of the dream and slowly meet, or move towards, whatever or wherever the fear emanates. Use the techniques described in the sections on Acting In and the answer dealing with recurring dreams.

If I dream I have sexual organs of the opposite sex, am I bisexual?
> Somehow my pants came right off. Nobody noticed, not even myself, until I was seated with knee up, heel in groin. Looking down, I noticed my legs were very smooth skinned and I had female sex organs. There was no pubic hair at all — Dan.

Dan is not bisexual or homosexual in his behaviour. But psychologically, everyone has the potential of the opposite sex. In most cases, such dreams show us dealing with this secondary side to our personality.

Do people dream in colour?
Examining the written record of thousands of dreams, most descriptions do not mention colour. When asked if they dream in colour, the majority of people find it difficult to answer. This is because for many there is no awareness of colour in dreams, except for occasional instances in which an object grabs our awareness because it is seen in colour. Some people, perhaps those with keen colour awareness while awake, do dream in colour more frequently. In dreams, colour is used to create mood. For instance, in many dreams where red appears, there is also heightened fear or anxiety.

How do we know things about people in our dreams?
As can be seen from the section on shared dreams, we often link

unconsciously with another person. In this way, we can know details that we have no idea about through our senses. We also have the ability to understand a great deal from subliminal awareness of the information we gather unconsciously from a person's body language and speech. This information may be presented in an intuitive dream.

How do you explain why some people never remember their dreams?
See section on *Does everybody Dream?*

What does it mean when you talk in your sleep?
> My boy friend frequently talks in his sleep and asks me things. When I wake up and ask him what he is talking about, he gets incredibly insistent and demands answers. Now, I usually tell him to go back to sleep and he does, but sometimes I think he is awake and things he says worry me. Why does he do this? — Debbie.

The answer to Debbie's question is probably that her boy friend carries worries into his sleep. Instead of talking them out with Debbie while awake, he wrestles with them in dreams. The worries then emerge in a way that concerns her more than if he were to approach them directly.

A more general understanding is explained under the question of *What makes me move or fight in my sleep?* Sleep talking ranges from the incomprehensible and gibberish to the other extreme of someone like American medium Edgar Cayce, who spoke fourteen million words in his sleep, all taken down by a secretary. Cayce — pronounced Kay-see — was able to tap the transcendent within and report information about health or any other subject asked about.[83]

In general, we may wake ourselves from sleep when we cry out from a troubling dream or sometimes in exciting dreams, such as making love.

Sleep talking occurs in REM sleep as well as non-REM sleep. In REM sleep, the person can usually remember some dream fragment linked with the talking. In non-REM sleep, no such memories can be found. An interesting description of sleep talking is given in *Tom Sawyer* after Tom witnessed a murder:

'Tom, you pitch around and talk in your sleep so much that you keep me awake about half the time'.

Tom blanched and dropped his eyes.

'It's a bad sign,' said Aunt Polly gravely. 'What you got on your mind, Tom?'

'Nothing. Nothing't I know of.' But the boy's hand shook so that he spilled his coffee.

Do creative people have more bizarre dreams?
An experiment was carried out at the University of Arizona, Tucson, USA, to see if creative people have more bizarre dreams. Dreams were collected from 126 undergraduates and rated for unusual features against controls. The experiment did not show that the undergraduates' dreams had any more unusual or imaginative features than anyone else. Perhaps the undergraduates were not particularly creative, but part of the Establishment.

Tests by other researchers show that we can extend our range of behaviour in dreams by becoming aware of habitual patterns expressed in them. For instance, if you are habitually passive in your dreams, becoming aware of this and deciding to express more fully in dreams and waking changes the habit.

Throughout history creative people have said they were given some of their most important ideas in dreams. Einstein dreamt about the Theory of Relativity in his teens. Elias Howe clearly 'saw' a design for making a functioning needle for his Singer sewing machine in a dream. William Blake was 'shown' how to create a new type of printing. There are too many others to list.

Why do some Christians say dreams are the Devil's work?
Many Fundamentalist Christians assert that we should all live in a way suggested by the Bible. However, their interpretation of the Bible is one which does not accept that dreams were taken seriously by the Jews and early Christians. The story of Joseph, the dream interpreter, is central to this as is the guidance given in dreams to the Apostles in the New Testament.

The Fundamentalists' fear is founded upon a rational difficulty. Many people base their life on superstitious beliefs, such as the power of an amulet. Fundamentalists want believers to abandon any such dependencies and place their trust in God, or rather in the interpretation they preach of God. Dreams are seen as another source of speculative dependency, and so are criticised. This has some historical context in that the early Christians had a long struggle with converts to eliminate their dependence on gods connected with dream incubation.

If you face this difficult question, it is important to define what is meant by God, and your personal relationship with Him. From there, you might have a clearer idea of a suitable direction for yourself.

How can I get answers to my life problems from my dreams?
Dreams are perhaps the most profoundly useful of any method of self-help. Each dream you have in some way informs you of what is important in your life and growth. Although occasionally a single dream will release an influence that will change your whole direction, usually it takes insight and involvement in many dreams to gain life changing-solutions.

Therefore, it is important to start a dream journal and extract as much as you can from at least one dream a week. Use the techniques described in Chapter Four. If possible, get a few friends to join you in your dream explorations. Such joint work is one of the most bonding and satisfying activities you can experience.

Dream Resources

Web Sites
Association for Research and Enlightenment
— http://www.are-cayce.com/
Association for the Study of Dreams
— http://www.dreamgate.com/dream/library
Calvin Hall
— http://ourworld.compuserve.com/homepages/hstein/
Casey Flyer — Links to dream sites
— http://members.aol.com/caseyflyer/fbnc/fbnc01.htm
Classical Adlerian Psychology
— http://ourworld.compuserve.com/homepages/hstein/
Dreamweavers Web
— http://www.dreamweavers.org/
Gayle Delaney's Site
— http://www.gdelaney.com
Gestalt Psychology
— http://www.gestalt.org/index.htm

Information about dream activities in the USA
http://www.dreamgate.com/dream/resources/offline.htm#centers
Online Dream Course
— http://www.outreach.org/dreams
Quantitative Study Of Dreams
— http://zzyx.ucsc.edu/~dreams/
Saybrook Faculty. Stanley Krippner
— http://www.saybrook.org/fackri.html
SleepNet
— http://www.sleepnet.com/
Tony Crisp's web pages
— http://dreamhawk.com/waves.htm

Yahoo web-page on dreams
— http://search.yahoo.com/bin/search?p=dreams

Useful Addresses

Association for the Study of Dreams (ASD). For further information, call (703) 242-8888. Address: POB 1600, E, Vienna, VA 22183. Contact Robert Gongloff at asdreams@aol.com

Association for Research and Enlightenment (ARE) with regional Edgar Cayce Dream Study Groups (800 368-2772 – USA and Canada only) Address: 215 67th Street, Virginia Beach, VA 23451. E-mail: are@are-cayce.com. Web site: http://www.are-cayce.com/

CAER, Rosemerryn, Lamorna, Penzance, Cornwall TR19 6BN. 0736 810530. One of Europe's longest established centres for personal development and training, located on the site of an Iron Age fortified settlement in the Celtic heart of Cornwall. E-mail: info@caer.co.uk. Web site: www.caer.co.uk.

C. G. Jung Institutes. A network of institutes offering libraries, bookstores, catalogues, groups, etc. C. G. Jung Institute of San Francisco Library, 2040 Gough Street, San Francisco, CA 94109. (415) 771-8055.

Maggie Peters, The Dreamwork Centre, Atcombe Court Wing, South Woodchester, Stroud, Glos GL5 5ER. Tel: 01453 872709. A professional training course for therapists and counsellors who would like to deepen their experience of working with clients' dreams.

Notes

1. (REM or NREM dreaming. The initials REM stand for 'rapid eye movement'. This refers to the fact, detailed later in the book, that in 1953 Aserinsky and Kleitman found rapid eye movements occurred while people slept. In 1957 the REM were linked with dreaming. Therefore sleep was observed to have two different phases, REM and NREM - non rapid eye movement, or non-REM. Later it was found that even during NREM sleep, a form of dreaming took place that is different to the REM dream with its pronounced imagery and drama.
2. I use the word spiritual to mean the sum total of all the linked interactions and dependencies within our body and the universe, enabling our personal existence. For instance we are dependent upon the sun for the growth of plant life. At the same time the interactions between sun, plant life and our body are a vital part of what enables our existence.
3. The *Concise Oxford Dictionary* defines intuition as 'immediate apprehension by the mind without reasoning'. I am using the word throughout the book to mean something slightly different. I do not mean intuition arising from feelings or fears without rational thought. The word is used to mean a direct knowing arising from a source beyond our senses or thinking. Sometimes writers use the word psychic to describe this, but the word psychic has associations I do not want to link with.
4. *Our Dreaming Mind* by Robert Van de Castle. Aquarian, London 1994.
5. Although at first sight this may run counter to common beliefs, if you look around and see that virtually every part of the world around you has been shaped and formed by human thought and effort, then it becomes more feasible.
6. *Altered States of Consciousness* edited by Charles C. Tart. The book is now unfortunately out of print, but should be easy to get through a book-search facility such as A&R Booksearch, High Close, Winnick Cross, Lanreath, Nr. Looe, Cornwall, PL13 2P. 01503 220246. Alternatively, try Dusty Books, The Old Woollen Mill, Shortbridge Street, Llanidloes, Powys SY18 6AD, Wales, UK. 01686 412515. Or: http://www.dustybooks.co.uk
7. For the complete article on Bullman's visit to Tart and his

other research, visit the *Electronic Telegraph* and search the archives for Tart or Bullman. http://www.telegraph.co.uk - Tart is Professor of Consciousness Studies at The University of Nevada in Las Vegas.
8. See Sacks's book *Awakenings*.
9. See Tony Crisp's books *Mind and Movement* and *Liberating the Body*. http://homepages.tesco.net/~waves/books.htm
10. Bob Holmes in The New Scientist – Archives, 26 April 1997.
11. This description of Tripp's hallucinations gives some idea of the level of his disturbance. "When one of the Walter Reed experts came in on a routine visit, Tripp shrank back in horror and disgust because it appeared that the doctor was wearing a suit made of crawling worms. On another occasion a nurse who was taking his blood pressure seemed to be drooling saliva all over the place. Insects were no longer seen as Disneyesque jokes, but as dangerous, threatening creatures. When opening a cupboard in the hotel to get a change of clothes he discovered that its interior was a mass of flames and for a moment inspired a panic that the hotel was on fire. His mood now changed sharply, and his normally benign personality exhibited signs of paranoia. The blaze in the cupboard was no longer accepted as being hallucinatory, but was a real fire started by one of the doctors to test him. When medical staff visited him he backed up against the wall in suspicion and terror." Quoted from *Landscapes of the Night*, by Christopher Evans. Victor Gollancz, 1983.
12. This only applies to a piece of holographic film, not to the holographic images one can buy in a shop or find on credit cards.
13. From *The Holographic Universe* by Michael Talbot. Grafton Press, 1991. ISBN O-24-13690-1.
14. See: *Brain and Perception : Holonomy and Structure in Figural Processing* by Karl H. Pribram. Lawrence Erlbaum Ass; Also, *The Creative Cosmos* by Ervin Laszlo and Karl H. Pribram. Floris Books. *Infinite Potential: The Life and Times of David Bohm* by F. David Peat. Addison Wesley Pub. *Wholeness and the Implicate Order* by David Bohm. Routledge.
15. Fictional names.
16. From. *Man and His Symbols* by Carl Jung. Aldus 1964.
17. From: *The Dancing Wu Li Masters - An Overview of the New Physics*, by Gary Zukav. Bantam Books, 1980.
18. Ibid.
19. Ibid.
20. See *Infinite Potential : The Life and Times of David Bohm* by F. David Peat. Addison Wesley Pub. Co. It shows how the exterior world is created out of collective thinking and feeling.
21. From *Dreams and Dreaming* by Norman MacKenzie. Bloomsbury Books 1989.

22. Ibid.
23. From *The Lightning Bird* by Lyall Watson. Hodder and Stoughton, 1982.
24. Recently evidence of much older writing has been found in Africa. See The Lightning Bird by Lyall Watson.
25. From *Dreams And Dreaming* by Norman MacKenzie.
26. Genesis 20.06.
27. Genesis 20.03.
28. The story of Adam was written in Hebrew, a language whose alphabetical characters each had a symbolic meaning, much as the characters alpha and omega mean something by themselves in the Greek alphabet. Therefore the words 'deep sleep', were 'thareddemah.' The roots of this word - according to Fred Myers - are rad and dam. In the English language we use the 'rad' root in such words as radiate, radium, radical. The Hebrew word "radah" means to rule to govern. The same root used as a "passive" verb means to be insensible, to be fast asleep, or to lose consciousness and control. The root 'dam' means to be connected through blood, similarity, kinship or identity. The whole word suggests a form of sleep in which the person loses self control and is directed by the will of another, perhaps as happens in hypnotic sleep.
29. Jung wrote that the conscious self raises prolific objections to becoming aware of unconscious experiences. It appears intent on blotting out spontaneous fantasy that might reveal something other than its own cherished defences and beliefs. It often takes firm determination to allow unconscious content. "In most cases the results of these efforts are not very encouraging at first. Moreover, the way of getting at the fantasies is individually different ... oftentimes the hands alone can fantasy; they model or draw figures that are quite foreign to the conscious." From Commentary in *Secret Of The Golden Flower* by Richard Wilhelm, commentary by Carl Jung. Routledge and Kegan Paul.
30. See: H. A. Sandison, A. M. Spencer, J. D. A. Whitelaw, *'The Therapeutic Value of Lysergic Acid Diethylamide in Mental Illness*. Grof, Stanislav, Realms of the Human Unconscious. Ling and Buckman, The use of LSD and Ritalin in the Treatment of Neuroses.
31. See *Prelogical Experience* by E. S. Tauber and Maurice S. R. Green.
32. From *Dreams And Dreaming* by Norman MacKenzie.
33. *LSD Psychotherapy* by W. V. Caldwell. Grove Press Inc. 1968
34. This listing is actually evolved from work done by Van Rhijn. Rhijn defined these levels.
35. See: Hall, Calvin S., *The Meaning of Dreams*, Harper and Row 1953. Hall, Calvin S., *Jungian Dream Interpretation*: A Handbook of Theory and Practice.
36. dtSearch can be obtained from www.dtsearch.com – e'mail: sales@

dtsearch.com or United Kingdom: ElectronArt Design Ltd. +44 (0) 181 983 8686 (voice and fax), uksales@dtsearch.com. Australia: Indigo Pacific Pty Ltd 61 2 9955 8000, Fax 61 2 9955 8511. australia@dtsearch.com. Canada: Gatierf Publications Ltd. 1-888-IT-FINDS, Fax (403) 293-6232. wright@gatpub.com. USA: 2101 Crystal Plaza Arcade, Suite 231, Arlington, Virginia 22202, USA. Toll-free Orders: 1-800-IT-FINDS (1-800-483-4637).

37. See: Van de Castle, Robert L., *Our Dreaming Mind*.

38. See *Living Your Dreams*, by Gayle Delaney. HarperCollins, 1996.

39. See note 30 for information about *dtSearch*.

40. For further information on journals see: Rainer, Tristine, *The New Diary*. Angus and Robertson, 1980. Also Capacchione, Lucia, *The Creative Journal*. Newcastle Pub. Co. 1993.

41. These questions were adapted from *The New Dream Dictionary* by Tony Crisp. *(Dream Dictionary* in USA). Little Brown 1995. http://homepages.tesco.net/~waves/books.htm.

42. See: *Living Your Dreams*, Gayle Delaney.

43. *Life Choices, Life Changes*, by Dina Glouberman. Thorsons, 1995.

44. 'Dream Detective' is adapted from *The New Dream Dictionary* by Tony Crisp *(Dream Dictionary* in USA). Little Brown 1995.

45. From *The Secret of The Golden Flower* by Richard Wilhelm, commentary by Carl Jung. Routledge and Kegan Paul.

46. There is not space to fully describe this technique in this book. For more information see Tony Crisp's books: Mind and movement – Liberating the Body – Instant Dream Book. Or visit this website http://homepages.tesco.net/~waves/prodream.htm

47. One of the most beautiful of surviving shrines to Aesculapius is at Epidaurus. It was built in the fifth century BC. Such centres were often of great size, and the one at Epidaurus took about 150 years to complete.

48. *Our Dreaming Mind* by Robert L. Van de Castle.

49. See: *Exploring The World of Lucid Dreaming* by Stephen LaBerge, and Howard Rheingold, Ballantine Books, 1990.

50. *The New Dream Dictionary* by Tony Crisp. Little Brown 1995. In the USA the book is titled *Dream Dictionary* and is published by Dell. The difference between the two titles is that *The New Dream Dictionary* is a revised and enlarged edition.

51. Published by Aldus 1964.

52. See *Escape From Freedom* by Erich Fromm, Avon Books, New York, 1965.

53. Quoted from Jung's commentary in Richard Wilhelm's *The Secret Of The Golden Flower*, Routledge and Kegan Paul.

54. *Experiment in Depth* was published by Routledge and Kegan Paul 1964. Martin was one of the early pioneers, along with Revd Leslie

Weatherhead, who started helping people to adequately explore their own dreams - i.e. without the psychiatrist.
55. *Sexual Dreams* by Dr. Gayle Delaney, Judy Piatkus, 1994.
56. Occasionally funeral dreams are expressing either an intuition about the health of the person buried, or are a means of practising feelings connected with losing them.
57. From *Love can Open Prison Doors*, by Star Daily.
58. Quoted from Jung's commentary in Richard Wilhelm's *The Secret Of The Golden Flower*.
59. From *LSD Psychotherapy* by W. V. Caldwell.
60. Paraphrased from *The Case for Reincarnation* by Dr. Leslie Weatherhead.
61. For a fuller examination of the question of rebirth see the book *Many Mansions* by Gina Cerminara, Signet Books.
62. Quoted from *Death Dreams* by Kenneth Paul Kramer and John Larkin, The Paulist Press.
63. Taken from P. H. Atwater's '*Coming Back to Life*' but quoted from an article in *Time Out*, November 7–14 1990 – *Nearly Departed*, by Colette Maud.
64. Dr. Morse's findings have been published in the American Medical Association's *American Journal of Diseases of Children* and in his book '*Closer to the Light*, Bantam. The quotes appeared in an article in *Time Out*, November 7–14 1990 – *Nearly Departed*, by Colette Maud.
65. From *The Politics of Experience and The Bird of Paradise,* by R. D. Laing, Penguin Books
66. As for instance in eating the body of Christ in mass.
67. Quoted from *Myself and I* by Constance Newland. Published by Frederick Muller Ltd, 1963.
68. Quoted from *Dream Power*, by Ann Faraday, Hodder & Stoughton Ltd, 1972
69. See Grof, Stanislav. *Realms of the Human Unconscious*, Souvenir Press 1979.
70. See a fuller description in *The Instant Dream Book*, by Tony Crisp, Chapter Nine in the section The Dream As Microscope, Telescope And Time Travel, C. W. Daniel Co. Ltd, 1984.
71. An urn used to hold the entrails of the embalmed person.
72. The sum total of past actions and attitudes that act to produce present experience, negative or positive.
73. Appeared in April 1995, Vol. 40(2) 161–175.
74. Published in Dreaming-Journal-of-the-Association-for-the-Study-of-Dreams; 1995. Sept Vol. 5(3) 189–198.
75. ie. patients who respond to treatment.
76. Quoted from PsycLIT Database Copyright 1996 American Psychological Assn, all rights reserved.
77. Record 769 of 3000 - PsycLIT Journal Articles 1/90–3/96 in the Bodleian Library, Oxford.
78. Record 676 of 3000 - PsycLIT

Journal Articles 1/90-3/96 in the Bodleian Library, Oxford.
79. J. B. Rhine was the person who introduced the words parapsychology and ESP – extra sensory perception. See: http://www.fpc.edu/academic/behave/psych/web93-1.htm
80. psychokinesis. This refers to the ability to move objects without obvious physical contact, by the power of mind.
81. From *The Holographic Universe* by Michael Talbot, Grafton Press, 1991.
82. See: *Dream Telepathy* by Ullman and Krippner, Turnstone 1973. Researched results of telepathy during dreaming.
83. See: *There Is a River*, by Thomas Sugrue, Dell. The first biography of Edgar Cayce.

Index

Active imagination, 50, 69
Adler, Alfred, 50–1, 54

Body in sleep, 24,

Castle, Robert van de, 55–6
Christ, 116
Christianity, 46

Delaney, Gayle, 55–6, 79
Dream Dictionary
  Aeroplane, 95
  Animals, 89
  Birds, 90
  Boat / Ship, 95
  Body, 83
  Buildings / home, 86
  Bus, 94
  Car, 94
  Clothes, 94
  Elements: Weather and
    Nature, 87
  Fire, 88
  Fish, 90
  Food and drink, 93
  Fruit, 92
  Money, 93
  Naked, 51, 94,
  Objects, 92
  Of murder, 113–15
  People, 81
  People events, 82
  Places / environments, 85
  Plants / Trees, 91
  Reptiles / Snakes, 90
  Seasons, 95
  Time, 95
  Train, 94
  Trees, 92
  Water, 88
Dreams
  Anxiety, 62, 141
  As pre-logical, 53
  Birth, 106, 120
  Body dreams, 15
  Children, 137–38
  Colour, 144
  Creative, 146
  Cultural views of, 35–6
  Definition of, 9
  Deprivations of, 27
  Destiny, 124
  Dramatising, 70–1
  Drugs, 53–5, 139
  Ego alien, 26
  Exploring, 64–8
  Facets of, 10–12
  Fantasy, 69–71
  Hallucinations, 23, 27
  History of, 42–58

INDEX

Illness, 126
Imagery of, 30
Information from, 32–5, 49
Inhabitants of, 99
Interpretation of, 45, 51, 62–4, 80–1
Language of, 23, 30, 53
Lucid – perforce, 78
Marriage and relationship, 128, 131, 135
Movements, 72
Of death or the dead, 101, 122–26, 136, 141
Philosophy of, 39–41
Problem solving, 14
Prophetic, 34, 140
Recurring, 100, 103, 142
Remembering, 59–61
Science and, 37–9
Self-regulation, 17, 29–30, 72, 98, 104
Supersenses, 16, 144
Symbolism in, 28, 30–2, 51
Telepathy in, 143
Themes, 55–6
Transformation, 115–18
Understanding, 22
Virtual reality of, 13
Working with, 48, 52, 61, 62–4, 98

Evil, 22

Freud, Sigmund, 47–8, 54
Fromm, Erich, 56, 107

Grof, Stanislav, 53, 132

Hall, Calvin, 55–6

Incubation, 46, 73–4

Journal, 61
Jung, Carl, 49–50, 54, 107, 117

Nightmares, 10–11, 19, 26, 100–3, 144

Out of body experience, 77

Paralysis, 21, 24–5
Perls, Fritz, 52
Physics, 33, 37–9

Sexuality, 48, 111–13, 131, 144
Sleep, 22
  Research, 24
  Movements during, 142
  Talking, 145

Tension, 72
Transcendent Self, 33–6, 40–1, 49, 130, 140
Trauma, 48